# You'll Leave This World with Your Butt Sewn Shut

# You'll Leave This World *with* Your Butt Sewn Shut

And OTHER LITTLE-KNOWN SECRETS, SHOCKING FACTS, *and* AMUSING TRIVIA ABOUT DEATH *and* DYING

ROBYN GRIMM

CASTLE POINT BOOKS
NEW YORK

www.castlepointbooks.com

The Castle Point Books trademark is owned by Castle Point Publishing, LLC.
Castle Point books are published and distributed by St. Martin's Publishing Group.

ISBN 978-1-250-32398-9 (trade paperback)
ISBN 978-1-250-32399-6 (ebook)

Edited by Jennifer Calvert
Design by Melissa Gerber

Images used under license by Shutterstock.com

Our books may be purchased in bulk for promotional, educational, or business use. Please
contact your local bookseller or the Macmillan Corporate and Premium Sales Department at
1-800-221-7945, extension 5442, or by email at MacmillanSpecialMarkets@macmillan.com.

First Edition: 2024

10 9 8 7 6 5 4 3 2 1

# CONTENTS

# A Peek Under Death's Robes

**H**AVE YOU EVER WONDERED HOW coroners can tell the time of death? Or whether funeral directors nap in their display caskets? Or how many people are killed by champagne corks each year? Well, wonder no more! *You'll Leave This World with Your Butt Sewn Shut* is here to take on your most pressing ponderances about death and dying. From the fascinating to the funny and even the oddly comforting, this tell-all book offers hundreds of facts to satisfy your morbid curiosity.

We all end up on the mortician's table eventually, so it's only natural to think about what the end entails. Page by page, you'll discover what Death's hiding under his robes and find answers to all the questions you don't know how to ask (and more than a few you never thought to). You'll learn why we fill funerals with flowers (it's not why you think), what happens to your medical implants and devices after you're dead, why morticians have the best makeup tips, and so much more.

Mostly curious about the butt bluntness in the book's title? Here's a tidbit to tide you over: Leaks happen—especially when the muscles that keep everything tightly shut stop working. But if you want to know more about how morticians handle all the ins and outs of the human body, you'll just need to read on. (Come on, you know you want to know.)

# CHAPTER 1

# The Dirt on Dying

SURE, HISTORY IS MORBIDLY FASCINATING, AND
MORTICIANS ARE UNFLAPPABLE MIRACLE WORKERS.
BUT TALES AND TIDBITS FROM THE CRYPT KEEPERS
CAN WAIT. YOU WANT THE COMPOST TEA, THE
DEETS ON DEATH ITSELF. SO LET'S GET INTO IT. THIS
CHAPTER SPILLS ALL OF THE GRIM REAPER'S SECRETS,
FROM THE MUNDANE TO THE MORTIFYING.

# DEATH BY NUMBERS

## DROPPING LIKE FLIES

More than 2.7 million people die in the United States in an average year. No getting around it—that's a lot of bodies. But if it's any consolation, that's only about 0.8 percent of the American population.

## GIRL WITH THE MERKITTEN TATTOO

The really disconcerting statistic is that 4,400 unidentified bodies are discovered each year. Roughly 1,000 of those bodies remain unidentified after a year. Really makes you think about getting some sort of unique body art, doesn't it?

## TASTES LIKE ELECTROLYTES

The top three causes of death, in order, are heart disease, cancer, and COVID-19. No surprises there. But the leading cause of *accidental* death is unintentional poisoning, which has to be a special kind of bummer. One minute, you're enjoying a sports drink; the next, you're dead—because it was actually antifreeze.

> "DEATH IS A VERY DULL, DREARY AFFAIR, AND MY ADVICE TO YOU IS TO HAVE NOTHING WHATEVER TO DO WITH IT."
>
> — W. SOMERSET MAUGHAM

# THE HUMAN BODY IS A NIGHTMARE

## ZOMBIES ARE REAL! (KIND OF)

There have been sixty-three cases of Lazarus Syndrome since the term was coined in 1982. That's where a person's blood spontaneously begins to recirculate after cardiac arrest—or, simply put, the medically dead come back to life. Imagine being the mortician minding your own business, prepping the embalming pump, when the stiff on your table sits up and starts wondering whether they're in an episode of *Criminal Minds*!

## A HAIR-RAISING EVENT

The dead can get goose bumps because the hair erector muscles automatically contract postmortem and make the hairs stand on end, making the corpse seem just as freaked out by their death as the person who found them probably was.

## GORY DETAIL

YES, YOU WILL POOP YOURSELF. AND WET YOUR PANTS. WHEN THE MUSCLES RELAX AFTER DEATH, SO DO THE BLADDER AND BOWELS. AND IT'S ONLY A MATTER OF TIME BEFORE THEY RELEASE WHATEVER THEY WERE HOLDING WHEN YOU DIED. LUCKILY, YOU WON'T BE ALIVE TO FEEL THE HUMILIATION OR DEAL WITH THE CLEANUP.

# THE TEA ON THE NDE

## GONE BUT NOT FORGETTING

Death occurs when the heart stops beating and starves the brain of oxygen. Within twenty seconds, the brain's cerebral cortex also flatlines. But new studies suggest that consciousness doesn't actually end there. In some patients, brain waves have been detected for as long as ten minutes after death.

## THE MIND IS A MYSTERY

Studies on near-death experiences—or NDEs, to those in the know—have given scientists a fresh perspective on the brain's role during and after death. But because they don't know the actual reasons behind the

persistent brain waves, that perspective varies wildly from scientist to scientist. Some think it's just chemical cocktails causing hallucinations, and some think it's evidence of life after death.

## I SEE LIVING PEOPLE

Studies can't explain, for example, why patients who've had their hearts restarted after cardiac death and lived to tell about it have reported watching the doctors work on them from outside of their bodies—with their doctors verifying the details they remember. (So, if you're a doctor, watch what you say around "dead" people.)

## CORROBORATING STORIES

People who have "crossed over," however briefly, report becoming pain free, flying, and seeing bright lights, tunnels, and loved ones more vividly than anything they had seen in life. But the really interesting and slightly hair-raising thing about these reports is how similar they are to each other. That's what gives them credence in the scientific community. (The warm fuzzies are enough to give them credence in the non-scientific community.)

## QUITE A TRIP

Those mystical visions are eerily similar to those of people who ingested hallucinogens linked to the neurotransmitter serotonin, such as psilocybin, LSD, DMT, and 5-MeO-DMT (aka the God Molecule). Some of these individuals were taking part in spiritual ceremonies. Others just really enjoyed the '70s.

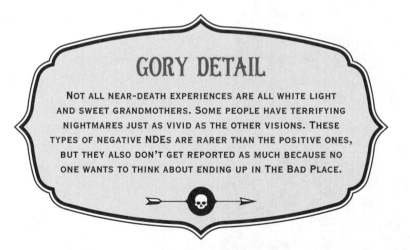

## GORY DETAIL

NOT ALL NEAR-DEATH EXPERIENCES ARE ALL WHITE LIGHT AND SWEET GRANDMOTHERS. SOME PEOPLE HAVE TERRIFYING NIGHTMARES JUST AS VIVID AS THE OTHER VISIONS. THESE TYPES OF NEGATIVE NDES ARE RARER THAN THE POSITIVE ONES, BUT THEY ALSO DON'T GET REPORTED AS MUCH BECAUSE NO ONE WANTS TO THINK ABOUT ENDING UP IN THE BAD PLACE.

## IN LIVING COLOR

Researcher Jimo Borjigin, who experimented on some very unlucky rats and watched their brain function, found that their brain waves surged after death, which could explain the virtual-reality-style postmortem visions. (Of course, it's hard to ask the rats what they experienced.)

........

## RATIONAL EXPLANATIONS

Scientists believe that one explanation for the surge in brain activity could be that it's the brain's last-ditch effort to save itself in the face of blood loss and oxygen deprivation. And, disappointingly, the cosmic tunnels could actually just be tunnel vision from reduced blood flow to the eyes.

........

## THIS IS YOUR LIFE

Researchers think that seeing your life flash before your eyes (which is, by the way, a real thing that happens) could be related to the activation of the temporal lobe of the brain, which is involved in memory and emotion.

"I'M SURE WHEREVER MY DAD IS, HE'S LOOKING DOWN ON US. HE'S NOT DEAD, JUST VERY CONDESCENDING."

—JACK WHITEHALL

14

# At Death's Door

## CALL AAA

CPR—or cardiopulmonary resuscitation, if you want to get technical— slows brain death by pumping some blood to the brain (about 15 percent of what it really needs to function), but it's kind of like jump-starting a dead car battery. Unless the heart starts beating on its own again, you're going to end up stranded in the grocery-store parking lot of life (aka the morgue).

## PLUMBING OR WIRING?

A heart attack and cardiac arrest are not the same thing. A heart attack occurs when blood flow to the heart is blocked (like when you've clogged your arteries with a few too many cheeseburgers). Cardiac arrest is when the heart stops beating entirely. The American Heart Association differentiates the two by saying that a heart attack is a circulation problem, and cardiac arrest is an electrical problem.

## CLOSE THE GENDER CPR GAP

Gender disparity has its grimy tentacles in everything—including life-saving CPR assistance. Women and men who drop at home are likely to get equivalent care. But dropping in public gives men an advantage: 45 percent of men receive care, compared with 39 percent of women. That means men are 1.23 times more likely to receive CPR from a bystander, which makes their chance of survival 23 percent higher than that of women.

## KILLING BRAIN CELLS

CPR might slow brain death, but it doesn't stop it. So the longer doctors perform life-saving measures, the more brain cells die off. That's why how long someone's been "down" matters. After about ten minutes, the odds are no longer in your favor.

## NO SMALL EFFORT

That doesn't mean there aren't exceptions to the rule. In 2011, fifty-four-year-old Howard Snitzer was revived after a massive heart attack by twenty first responders taking turns during ninety-six minutes of CPR. (Anyone familiar with volunteer first-aid squads knows the real miracle was having twenty people on the squad.)

# UNMISTAKABLE SIGNS OF DEATH

## LAST HURRAH

*Grey's Anatomy* fans will be familiar with this tidbit (RIP Mark Sloan): In the last days of life, a previously feeble and definitely dying person can have a sudden burst of energy and liveliness, referred to as *terminal lucidity*, or, more colloquially, "the surge before death," before the final crash. It can feel like a final gift or a cruel fake-out, depending on your perspective.

........

## THE TWILIGHT MOAN

When breathing becomes intermittent toward the end, air passing over very relaxed vocal cords can make the dying person moan every thirty seconds or so. The good news is, it's not an indication of pain or distress. The bad news is, it's deeply unsettling.

### · DUMB WAYS TO DIE ·

Speaking of surging energy: The odds of dying by energy drink are low, but they're not zero. One gamer's pancreas started digesting itself after he chugged twelve cans in a row. Incredibly, he lived (thanks to immediate medical intervention), but the Center for Science in the Public Interest has linked over thirty deaths to the reinvigorating drinks.

## THE END CREDITS

More unsettling is the "death rattle"—or, technically, "end-stage wet respirations." When the muscles of the lungs and trachea grow weak, and saliva and mucus build up in the airways, breath passing through the fluids can cause a rattling sound. This is considered a sign of imminent death.

## THE TELLTALE . . . LEGS

When death is drawing near, blood circulation begins to slow, creating obvious signs of the inevitable, such as the limbs taking on a blotchy purple or bluish hue. In fact, some medical practitioners tell loved ones to watch the patient's legs, which will "look dead" at the end.

## NOW IT'S OFFICIAL

You're not considered *dead* dead until a healthcare provider observes a lack of pulse, breathing, reflexes, and pupillary reaction to bright light. That's called *cardiac death*, and at that point, you're officially dead.

"WHAT I WANT AT MY FUNERAL IS AN ACTUAL BOXING REFEREE TO DO A COUNT, AND AT FIVE, JUST WAVE IT OFF AND SAY, 'HE'S NOT GETTING UP.'"

—GARRY SHANDLING

## PLUGGED IN

If the patient meets just one out of the four criteria—namely, having a pulse—they'll be declared *brain-dead* and kept on a ventilator until the family decides to unplug them. Recovery isn't an option, though. The only real difference is the ability to donate organs, which are kept viable via the ventilator.

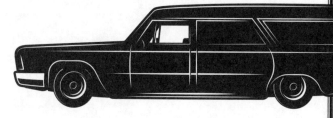

## DEATH BY CROSSING STATE LINES

In New York and New Jersey, families can reject the concept of brain death if it goes against their religious beliefs. To them, their loved one is alive as long as their body is still functioning. This means that a person can be declared dead in some states but considered alive in others. (That's got to be tricky at tax season.)

## NOT A COMMON OCCURRENCE

Contrary to what every television drama in need of a plot twist would have you believe, brain deaths are pretty rare. Only 1 percent of all deaths qualify. That's part of the reason that organ donations are hard to come by.

## GORY DETAIL

WHEN YOU'RE DEALING WITH DEATH ON THE FLY AS AN EMT OR PARAMEDIC, THE CRITERIA FOR INTERVENTION ARE A LITTLE LESS SUBTLE. THEY ABIDE BY THE FIVE SIGNS OF IRREVERSIBLE DEATH WHEN DECIDING WHETHER RESUSCITATION IS AN OPTION: DECAPITATION, DECOMPOSITION, POSTMORTEM LIVIDITY, POSTMORTEM RIGIDITY, AND BURNED BEYOND RECOGNITION.

## FAMOUS LAST WORDS

EMTs and other healthcare providers will tell you that some of the most common phrases they hear before someone dies are "Something's not right" and "I feel like I'm going to die." They might roll their eyes at a patient's Google-inspired self-diagnosis, but they'll hop to if they hear those words.

## THE ACTUAL WALKING DEAD

There's a rare psychiatric condition called Cotard's Syndrome—aka "Walking Corpse Syndrome"—that makes individuals believe they are already dead, do not exist, or have lost their vital organs. But since they're still walking around in the world, and cognitive dissonance is a powerful thing, they also believe themselves immortal.

# As the Lights Go Out

## CELLS GO AT THEIR OWN PACE

The actual act of dying begins when your body doesn't get enough oxygen to keep your cells alive. Cell death begins within five minutes of oxygen deprivation. And different cells die at different speeds. So although you may technically be dead, it's not like flipping a switch.

...........

## SAY HI TO AUNT TRUDY

Your brain and nerve cells are the first to go when you stop breathing. They last three to seven minutes. When your brain cells die, you can experience changes in your consciousness, perception, memory, and emotions—including hallucinations. That could explain why some people come back from near-death experiences having had visions of particular people or places. (Then again, you never know.)

## · DUMB WAYS TO DIE ·

In 2011, Fagilyu Mukhametzyanov died of shock from waking up at her own funeral after having "died" of a heart attack. (Did someone forget to the lock the doors to the Underworld?) The forty-nine-year-old screamed (reasonably), her eyes fluttered, and then she was dead again.

## GORY DETAIL

In 1601, Danish astronomer Tycho Brahe died of a burst bladder because he was too polite to excuse himself during a royal dinner. After hours of holding it, he found he couldn't go at all. And because medicine mostly consisted of leeches and opium in those days, he never did find relief.

## NOT-SO-BLEEDING HEART

The gradual death of your heart cells is what causes your heartbeat to slow, become irregular, and/or stop altogether. Your skin will get pale, grow cold, and take on a lovely blue hue. Or it would be lovely, if it weren't a harbinger of death.

## DON'T SMOKE 'EM

If your lung cells die early on (e.g., it's your smoking habit that kills you), breathing can become shallow, rapid, noisy, and startlingly hard to come by. Then go the abilities to swallow and cough. But after brain death, it takes the lungs about an hour to die. It feels like that resilience would be handier while you're still breathing.

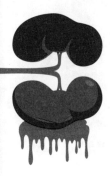

## BETTER DEAD THAN DELIRIOUS

Your kidneys also die about an hour after your brain. Because the kidneys filter out toxins, and their death can cause some issues premortem—like swelling, sleeplessness, nausea, and confusion—that's really the best-case scenario.

## A TERMINAL BLOODBATH

The liver is responsible for clotting, so when its cells die, things can get bloody. But if you're already dead and your blood has stopped circulating, you're all good. Minus the being dead part.

## KEEP ON KEEPING ON

Skin, tendons, heart valves, and corneas can keep functioning for a whole day after death. White blood cells hold on even longer—almost three days.

"IF DEATH IS ANYTHING LIKE SLEEP, IT'S GOING TO BE INTERESTING WHEN I FREQUENTLY RISE FROM THE GRAVE TO PEE."

—BRIDGER WINEGAR

# A FEAST FOR THE SENSES

### STARING INTO THE ABYSS

One of the first signs of death (aside from the lack of pulse, obviously) is when the eyes cloud over. That horrifying milky-white stare is due to a lack of fluid and oxygen flowing to the corneas, and it can happen in as little as ten minutes if the eyes are open.

### IN YOUR EYELINE

When the eyes are not closed after death and the sclera is exposed to air, it can produce *tache noire de la sclérotique*, which is French for "black spot of the sclera" but is really a freaky reddish-brown line across the eyeball.

## GORY DETAIL

WHEN YOUR BLOOD STOPS CIRCULATING AND YOUR BLOOD PRESSURE BOTTOMS OUT, YOUR EYEBALLS FLATTEN. (LEST YOU THOUGHT THOSE NIGHTMARISH HALLOWEEN DECORATIONS WITH THEIR PERFECTLY ROUND EYEBALLS POPPING OUT WERE ACCURATE PORTRAYALS OF THE DEAD.)

## EYES WIDE OPEN

Speaking of which . . . your eyes don't automatically close when you die. In fact, a lot of people die with their eyes open because, when the muscles of the face relax, it can cause the eyelids to fall back. So those touching scenes in movies where the hero gently closes his dead sidekick's lids are spot-on.

## FRESH GOSS 'TIL THE END

Your hearing is the last sense to go when you die, which is helpful for catching any last-minute deathbed confessions from loved ones.

### · DUMB WAYS TO DIE ·

Plastic straws may be deadly to turtles, but the alternatives have their own drawbacks. In July of 2019, 60-year-old Elena Struthers-Gardner died when she fell on the stainless-steel straw of her mason jar–style drinking glass in her own kitchen. It went through her left eye socket and into her brain. (Plastic straws are looking better and better.)

# BODIES ON THE MOVE

## WALKING (OR TALKING) DEAD VIBES

Dead people have been known to moan, groan, and otherwise vocalize. This is more common when someone has had (unsuccessful) life-saving measures taken on their behalf. Doing CPR pumps their defunct lungs and stomach full of air, which comes back out when the body is moved.

## A CREEPY CHEMICAL REACTION

Speaking of excessively creepy and unnecessary biological processes, muscles can twitch after death. The cause is the postmortem release of chemicals in the nerves as they die off. The result is scaring the living hell out of even the most experienced morticians.

## GORY DETAIL

ADDING TO THE SPINE-CHILLING EFFECT OF POSTMORTEM MOVEMENT IS THE FACT THAT CADAVERIC SPASMS CAN INDICATE A TRAUMATIC DEATH. THE MUSCLES USED MOST WHEN DEATH OCCURRED LOCK TIGHTER THAN THOSE UNDERGOING NORMAL RIGOR, THEN THEY SPASM WHEN FINALLY RELAXED. A HORRIFYING EXAMPLE: IF YOU WERE FRANTICALLY CLINGING TO A CLIFF'S EDGE BEFORE FALLING, YOUR FINGERS MIGHT SPASM AFTER DEATH.

# GET 'EM WHILE YOU CAN

## THE ORGAN SHUFFLE

If you're an organ donor, transplant surgeons have just thirty minutes from the moment you die to whip out those organs before they follow suit. From there, the surgeons have six hours to get the organs into their new (and hopefully longer-living) humans.

.........

## SKIN CARE SAVES LIVES

Skin grafts taken from the dead have a much more forgiving window of success—up to twelve hours. If only skin were that forgiving *premortem!* But at least that twelve-step skin care routine of yours can benefit the next guy.

## · DUMB WAYS TO DIE ·

In 2011, Philip A. Contos died in a motorcycle accident during a protest of New York State's helmet laws. The medical examiner said that, had Phil been wearing his helmet, he would have certainly survived. Don't be like Phil.
Wear your brain bucket.

## NO TIME TO WAIT

If waiting to see a doctor tests your patience, you won't believe what it's like to wait on an organ. An average of 100,000 people are in line for life-saving organ transplants in the United States, with another added every ten minutes. It can take three to five years to find a match, and twenty-two people die waiting every day.

## SECONDHAND EYEBALLS

A dead body has a surprising amount of life to give. One organ donor can save eight lives, and that doesn't include the seventy-five people who can benefit from their tissue donations (e.g., heart valves, bones, tendons, veins, and skin). Sure, it might be weird to think about someone else seeing the world through your baby blues, but it's also a way better gift than any whiskey stones or gift cards.

## PUT YOUR LIVER TO GOOD USE

Speaking of which, a whopping 95 percent of Americans are in favor of organ donation, but only 58 percent are registered. That's like buying a bag of spring mix with the best of intentions every week just to watch it get brown, soggy, and eventually tossed, unused, into the garbage. (Register today!)

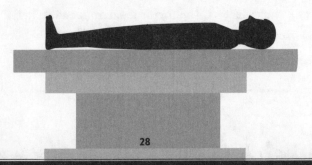

# SEE YOU LATER, OVULATOR

### PERIOD, AS IN STOP

Dying may be the only way to stop your period early. Instead of flowing out like other bodily fluids, menstrual blood stops moving and coagulates just a few minutes into the decomp process.

.........

### AN EVERLASTING CATCHALL

The average tampon isn't biodegradable, so on the off chance the mortician doesn't remove it before you're buried (an unlikely event), it'll outlast everything but your bones. But don't feel too bad—even tampons made with 100 percent cotton take five to six months to decompose.

.........

### OH, BABY

Babies still in utero can survive their mother's death if they are delivered within four minutes of cardiac arrest, but their odds of survival go down with every week of prematurity. Those who die in utero remain that way unless the family chooses to have them delivered and buried separately.

"ONLY THE
YOUNG
DIE GOOD."
—OLIVER HERFORD

## GORY DETAIL

DYING DOESN'T NECESSARILY GET A PERSON OUT OF GIVING BIRTH, BUT THE PROCESS WILL BE FAR LESS PAINFUL. IF THEY DIE WHILE STILL PREGNANT, THE GASES FROM DECOMPOSITION CAN PUSH THE FETUS OUT IN WHAT'S HORRIFYINGLY CALLED A "COFFIN BIRTH."

### STILL GUESSING

Stillbirths are infant deaths that occur after the fetus has reached twenty-four weeks. (Before that, it's deemed a miscarriage.) These deaths are shocking on their own, but even more so because doctors often can't uncover the cause.

### RIGOR-LESS

When infants and young children die, their bodies often don't display signs of rigor mortis. This might be because of their smaller muscle mass, or it might be some small mercy from the Universe for their loved ones.

# DEATH IN FOUR ACTS

## DEATH IS JUST A PHASE

Rigor mortis is the most well-known "mortis," but it isn't the only one. The body goes through four phases of death before decomposition sets in: pallor mortis, algor mortis, *then* rigor mortis, and finally livor mortis. These stages help forensic experts determine time of death.

.........

## THE VAMPIRE EFFECT

Pallor mortis is the stage in which blood stops pumping through the capillaries, draining the color from the body and making you look like a sun-starved vampire (sans glitter, if your preferred genre is "sexy undead creatures"). It occurs within the first fifteen to twenty minutes of death.

## GORY DETAIL

IT ACTUALLY TAKES A WHILE TO BECOME "COLD AND DEAD."
DURING ALGOR MORTIS, THE BODY (WHICH OBVIOUSLY CAN'T COOL
OR HEAT ITSELF ANYMORE) LOSES NEARLY 1.5°F EVERY HOUR
AFTER DEATH. BUT IT ONLY SEEMS COLD IN COMPARISON TO THE
BODY'S USUAL 98.6°F TEMPERATURE. LIKE MEAT LEFT OUT ON THE
COUNTER—WHICH WE BASICALLY ARE AT THAT POINT—THE BODY
STOPS COOLING WHEN IT REACHES AMBIENT TEMPERATURE.

# NO LONGER A WORKING STIFF

### FREEZE FRAME

Rigor mortis (the hallmark stiffening of a body from which the spectacularly descriptive slang term "stiff" sprang) is caused by chemical bonds in the fibers of the muscles. It starts in the face two hours after death and spreads over the rest of the body in four to six hours.

### JUST GIVE IT TIME

Much like being alive or feeling hangry, rigor is a temporary state. It lasts for about twenty-four hours after death, peaking at thirteen hours, and starts to dissipate as the chemical bonds in the muscles break down.

### BURNING BRIDGES

The main cause of rigor mortis is depletion of the cells' energy molecule, adenosine triphosphate (ATP). ATP separates actin–myosin bridges within the muscles so they can relax. Without it, the bridges lock in place. When the muscles relax again, it's not because ATP got back from its lunch break. It's because decomp burns the bridges.

## WHAT TIME IS IT?

Yes, forensic experts can use rigor to estimate time of death. But it's not nearly as easy as every crime show ever on television would have you believe. (Who would have guessed, right?) Many factors affect the onset and duration of rigor mortis, including ambient temperature, body weight, clothing, illness, physical activity, and cause of death. Getting it right requires some serious problem-solving skills.

## PASS THE TUNA ROLL

Sushi lovers might want to look away from this one. Sushi chefs age their fish to let rigor pass so that you don't break your jaw trying to chew it. (But, just like with aging a good steak, it does also make the fish more flavorful.)

## RELAX THOSE MUSCLES

There are two different periods of muscle relaxation—one before rigor and one after. They're called primary and secondary flaccidity, because no one has a sense of humor like a scientist.

"DEATH IS JUST NATURE'S WAY OF TELLING YOU TO SLOW DOWN."

—DICK SHARPLES

## NO NEED FOR NAIL CLIPPERS

Contrary to popular belief, your hair and fingernails do not continue to grow after you die. The truth is much more unnerving: it only seems like your hair and nails have grown because your skin retracts as it dehydrates during secondary flaccidity, exposing what was underneath.

## BUT MAYBE A SHAVE

That's also why men who were clean-shaven at death seem to have a five o'clock shadow hours later. Only in death can you truly master the "sexy stubble" look.

## AND A LITTLE LIP PLUMPER

Your lips also dehydrate and retract, exposing more of your teeth and making you look like someone imitating a beaver while telling a bad dad joke.

> "DEATH,
> HAIR AND
> FINGERNAILS
> CONTINUE
> TO GROW, BUT
> PHONE CALLS
> TAPER OFF."
> —JOHNNY CARSON

# LIVOR, NOT LIVER

## A PUDDLING OF BLOOD

Beginning in as little as thirty minutes after the blood stops circulating, gravity takes over, allowing the blood to pool in the lowest areas (wherever those might be, depending on the manner of death). The process is called *livor mortis*.

## SOOTHING MOVEMENT

Changing the body's position in the early stages of livor mortis can move the pools of blood—kind of like one of those liquid-motion toys you played with as a kid. (Plus, the blood creates a similarly cool purple marbling effect under the skin.)

### GORY DETAIL

AFTER ABOUT SIX HOURS, THE BLOOD COAGULATES, AND LIVOR MORTIS IS "FIXED." THOSE AREAS WHERE THE BLOOD HAS POOLED WILL LOOK BLACK BECAUSE THE DEOXYGENATED HEMOGLOBIN IN THE BLOOD HAS GONE DARK. SO IF YOU FIND A BODY FACE DOWN BUT WANT TO HAVE A VIEWING, YOU BETTER TURN IT OVER QUICK. MORTUARY MAKEUP CAN ONLY DO SO MUCH!

## ERECTIONS HAPPEN

Postmortem erections don't necessarily mean that the person was having a good time when they died. If the body is lying face down at the time of death, and blood pools at the lowest areas, one of those areas might be the penis.

## COME AGAIN?

That's not the only way to get it up after death. Rigor mortis can also cause the penis to become erect. The decedent can even ejaculate—sort of. What was previously thought to be ejaculate is actually a mixture of bodily fluids seeping from the prostate gland. Sexy, right?

"DEATH IS A DELIGHTFUL HIDING PLACE FOR WEARY MEN."

—HERODOTUS

## THE FAMILY LINE CONTINUES

Although sperm might be mixed with those other bodily fluids, they render it pretty ineffectual (and super gross). But it *is* possible to surgically retrieve viable sperm for up to twenty-four hours postmortem.

# Happy Endings

## ANGEL LUST ISN'T HEAVENLY

Death erections—creatively labeled "angel lust" by some—are most common in hanging deaths but can also be seen after fatal gunshots to the brain and violent death by poisoning. So they've become associated with quick and brutal deaths. Scientists think the phenomenon has to do with pressure on the cerebellum.

..........

## POSTMORTEM PETIT MORT

Men aren't the only ones who can be aroused without being roused. Women who are brain dead and being kept on a ventilator can orgasm through sacral-nerve stimulation. The real question here isn't how, but why, which is why this is theoretical and not practical science.

## · DUMB WAYS TO DIE ·

In general, sex is great for the body. It boosts the immune system, helps you sleep, and increases happy chemicals in the brain. But some people take it too far—namely, the hundreds of Americans whose lives are claimed by autoerotic asphyxia each year. After all, it's tricky to invoke a safe word when you can't speak. (RIP David Carradine.)

# IT'S A PROCESS

### LIKE A SWISS CLOCK...

Regularity isn't an issue after death (as evidenced also by the postmortem colon cleanse). The body predictably cycles through five phases of decomposition: autolysis (cell breakdown or self-digestion), bloat, active decay, advanced decay, and skeletonization.

### ...WITH A SNOOZE BUTTON

That said, there's no standard timeline for the decomposition process. Its regularity depends on a few factors: namely, the size of the body, the temperature of the body, moisture levels, oxygen levels, pH levels, and whether it's above or below ground.

"ONE CAN SURVIVE EVERYTHING, NOWADAYS, EXCEPT DEATH, AND LIVE DOWN EVERYTHING EXCEPT A GOOD REPUTATION."

—OSCAR WILDE

### AND AN INTERNAL POWER SOURCE

If the body makes its way to a funeral home within forty-eight hours (most do) and is embalmed, the decomp clock doesn't stop, but it slows down long enough for the body to be whipped into shape (kind of literally—see Chapter 3) and stay powdery fresh through a viewing (about a week). Any longer than forty-eight hours, and things get tricky for even the most talented mortuary makeup artists.

# PHASE 1: SELF-DIGESTION

### PASS THE ANTACID

Autolysis—or, delightfully, self-digestion—begins right after death and lasts roughly six days. As oxygen stops circulating, anaerobic organisms begin to break the body down into organic acids and gases.

### AN OCCASIONALLY TASTY PROCESS

Autolysis doesn't just occur in dead bodies. It's also the reason why aged cheese, wine, and steak taste so good. Just like in the human body, the enzymes in their cells break down the proteins, fats, and sugars into smaller and more flavorful molecules.

## GORY DETAIL

BACTERIA FROM THE PANCREAS DIGEST THE PANCREAS AND THEN MOVE ON TO THE REST OF THE ORGANS. BUT THE BACTERIA DON'T STOP THERE! WHILE THEY'RE EATING YOUR ORGANS, THEY RELEASE GAS, CAUSING THE BODY TO BLOAT AND THEN LIQUEFY.

## AN UNMISTAKABLE SCENT

On the other, less appetizing, hand, autolysis is the reason why you know a dead body when you smell it. The enzymes in the cells release gases and liquids that cause the body to bloat, leak, and, well, stink.

## THEY GOT THE NAMES RIGHT

The molecules produced by the bacteria breaking down the amino acids ornithine and lysine in a body have two of the most fitting names in all of science: putrescine and cadaverine, respectively.

### · DUMB WAYS TO DIE ·

Bacteria will get you either way, but better that they get you after you're dead than be the cause of your death. Yet history is filled with idiots dying from treatable infections. French composer Jean-Baptiste Lully, for example, died in 1653 after stabbing himself in the foot with his conductor's staff. He refused an amputation because of his love of dance, and the infection killed him.

# PHASE 2: BLOAT

### LIKE A REALLY GROSS BALLOON

Thanks to those overzealous, cannibalistic bacteria, bloating can begin in as little as two days after death and lasts a couple of weeks. And if you think post-Thanksgiving bloat is bad, you ain't seen nothing yet. The body can actually double in size during this phase. So, really, it's closer to the balloons in the Thanksgiving-day parades.

### NO FOOD WASTED

The good bacteria in your digestive tract don't really care that you're dead—they've got a job to do. So while the parasitic bacteria are breaking down amino acids, the digestive bacteria continue to work on breaking down your last meal.

## GORY DETAIL

AS THE BODY FILLS WITH GAS, IT SWELLS AND IS DISTORTED BY THE PRESSURE, WHICH CAN CAUSE THE SKIN TO CRACK AND LEAK FLUIDS, AND THE EYES AND TONGUE TO BULGE OUT. AND IT'S NOT JUST THE ABDOMEN AND CHEST THAT PUFF UP—THE SCROTUM IS ALSO ONE OF THE MOST INFLATED AREAS.

## MITIGATING FACTORS

Temperature, humidity, oxygen level, clothing, body position, cause of death, and embalming can all affect the length and severity of the bloating. For example, colder temperatures can slow down or prevent bloating (hence, refrigerated morgues), while warmer temperatures can speed it up or make it more severe. You don't want to see a body that's been sitting out in a hot swamp!

........

## BLOATING OR FLOATING

Bodies that reach this bloat phase underwater (for whatever totally not-mob-related reasons) can resurface as the gas inflates them. These are diplomatically called "refloats" by rescue workers.

........

## GAS MASKS EXIST FOR A REASON

The bloat phase ends when the gases escape through the openings or cracks of the body, causing it to deflate. But when those gases release—through whichever orifice or fissure they can—you'll want to be in a different zip code. The smell is, as you'd expect, like a combination of fart, vomit, and decay.

"GOOD. A WOMAN WHO CAN FART IS NOT DEAD."

LAST WORDS OF MARIE-THÉRÈSE LOUISE DE SAVOIE-CARIGNAN, PRINCESSE DE LAMBALLE

# PHASE 3: ACTIVE DECAY

## COVER YOUR MOUTH

The maggots that feed on the corpse are mostly from blowflies and flesh flies, which can smell a dead body from more than 6 miles away thanks to the methane, carbon dioxide, nitrogen, and hydrogen sulfide the body releases. The flies lay their eggs in natural openings (read: eye sockets, mouth, and other orifices you don't want to think about) or wounds, and the larvae hatch within twenty-four hours.

## GET THE BLEACH

You know when you pull back the carpet in a new house and find suspicious stains? Blood might not be the worst possibility! The fluids that seep out of the body during decomposition are called "purge fluids," and they can stain the soil or surface where a body lies. Purge fluid can also attract more insects, microorganisms, and even animals to help the process of decay along.

## GORY DETAIL

ACTIVE DECAY IS THE ULTIMATE DIET—INSTEAD OF EATING THINGS, THINGS EAT YOU. THIS IS THE STAGE WHEN THE BODY LOSES MOST OF ITS MASS AS FLUIDS AND GASES LEAK OUT AND MAGGOTS GO TO WORK ON THE TISSUE. A BODY CAN LOSE UP TO 80 PERCENT OF ITS INITIAL WEIGHT DURING ACTIVE DECAY.

## GORY DETAIL

"GRAVE WAX" ISN'T SOME SORT OF ADD-ON SERVICE PROVIDED BY THE CEMETERY. THE SOAP-LIKE FILM—CALLED *ADIPOCERE*—COVERS SOME BODIES WHEN FAT DECAYS UNDER WET, OXYGEN-STARVED CONDITIONS (LIKE AT THE MUDDY BOTTOM OF A LAKE).

> "AT MY AGE, I DO WHAT MARK TWAIN DID. I GET MY DAILY PAPER, LOOK AT THE OBITUARIES PAGE, AND IF I'M NOT THERE, I CARRY ON AS USUAL."
>
> —PATRICK MOORE

## NOT THOSE WORMS

When you think of "becoming worm food," you probably imagine earthworms eating away at you. But they're the latecomers to the decay buffet, preferring to wait until organic matter (you) more closely resembles the soil around it. The worms the phrase refers to are actually maggots.

## COMING UP CORPSE FLOWERS

Speaking of the wonders of nature, there's a massive flower that only blooms once every 7 to 10 years, for only 24 to 48 hours each time, and can grow as much as 10 feet tall. But its real claim to fame is that it smells like a dead body. Its name? The corpse flower, appropriately.

# PHASE 4: ADVANCED DECAY

### THE LAST OF US

When a body reaches advanced decay, most of the soft tissues have already decomposed, and only bones, hair, cartilage, ligaments, and sticky residue from decomposition are left. It's your basic *Tales from Crypt* situation.

·········

### LIKE LONG-FORGOTTEN LEFTOVERS

If that's not creepy enough, the decomp byproducts then turn leathery and black—just to hammer home that the body is done and ready to give way to the bones.

·········

### CHANGING OF THE GUARD

Like the second shift clocking in for the night, more pernicious insects like beetles and certain types of flies arrive during this stage to finish the job. They'll chew on and process the tougher materials and use the increasingly visible bones as a nesting site for their larvae.

## THE GRASS IS GREENER, EVENTUALLY

Contrary to popular belief, dead bodies aren't great for plant life. If a decaying body is on or in soil rather than in a casket, you'll notice the surrounding vegetation also dying thanks to all the things that have oozed out of the body, causing the same effect as fertilizer burn. But, in a few years, the remains will basically become compost, and the grass will come back even greener.

## NO SKELETON FOR YOU

If the body is covered in grave wax, decomp could end here. This substance preserves what's left of the body and protects it from reaching the final stage: skeletonization.

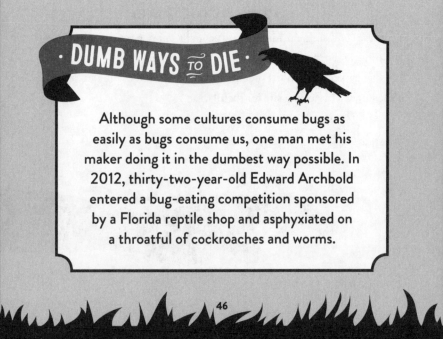

## DUMB WAYS TO DIE

Although some cultures consume bugs as easily as bugs consume us, one man met his maker doing it in the dumbest way possible. In 2012, thirty-two-year-old Edward Archbold entered a bug-eating competition sponsored by a Florida reptile shop and asphyxiated on a throatful of cockroaches and worms.

# PHASE 5: SKELETONIZATION

### ALL DRIED UP

Skeletonization also goes by a far less creative name: *dry decay*. That one's pretty self-explanatory. At this stage, the body is like your stomach after the flu: it has nothing left to purge.

### DUST TO DUST

Despite seeming especially fragile in life—especially where teenagers are involved—bones take the longest of any body part to break down: around twenty years. The process is called *diagenesis*.

### LIKE A DOG WITH A . . .

The protein in the bones is the first to go, which leaves them vulnerable to cracking and flaking from moisture, freezing and thawing, erosion, and wild meat-eating creatures. (Yes, they enjoy a good bone as much as the average German Shepherd.)

## YOU AND THE DINOSAURS

Of course, there are plenty of exceptions to the rule that bones eventually break down too. (Otherwise, what would archaeologists do with their time?) Dry soil is naturally filled with bone-strengthening minerals that can help preserve them for future generations to ogle on social media.

## NOW THEY STOP?

Despite spending our lives fending off tooth decay, teeth don't decompose after death. The bacteria that cause decay helpfully retire from duty (i.e., become inactive) when you die.

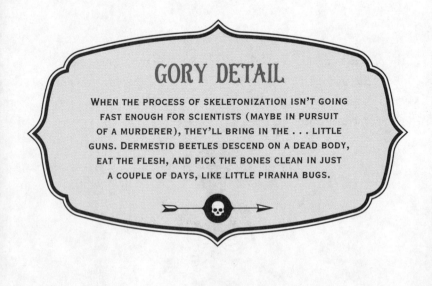

## GORY DETAIL

WHEN THE PROCESS OF SKELETONIZATION ISN'T GOING FAST ENOUGH FOR SCIENTISTS (MAYBE IN PURSUIT OF A MURDERER), THEY'LL BRING IN THE . . . LITTLE GUNS. DERMESTID BEETLES DESCEND ON A DEAD BODY, EAT THE FLESH, AND PICK THE BONES CLEAN IN JUST A COUPLE OF DAYS, LIKE LITTLE PIRANHA BUGS.

# YOU CAN'T STOP DECOMP (WITH A COFFIN)

## BUYING TIME

A body buried in a coffin starts to break down within a year and will probably fully decompose before it hits double digits. By springing for bells and whistles like lining and sealing, you can literally buy yourself more time. But for what?

## DECAY PERSISTS

People like to think they can keep the worms at bay. But just like Tupperware can't keep your leftovers fresh forever, even the most perfectly airtight coffin set in a concrete burial vault won't keep nature from taking its course.

## ANTIBIOTICS REALLY WORK

One thing that might buy your body more time is what you put into it before death. Chemotherapy and antibiotics used prior to biting the dust can kill off some of the bacteria involved in the decomp process.

"I INTEND TO LIVE FOREVER, OR DIE TRYING."

—GROUCHO MARX

# WE'RE ALL MEAT IN THE END

## CATS WILL EAT YOUR FACE

Under dire circumstances, even humans have been known to eat each other. So why do you think a hungry cat (or dog) wouldn't? They might wait until things get really bad, but they might not. It depends on the pet, and it has more to do with instinct than affection.

## DOGS WILL DO IT SOONER

Dogs are actually more likely to dig in shortly after your death. Experts think one reason for this might be that the dog accidentally ingests a bit of their favorite human during attempts to wake them, and then instinct takes over. But that might be wishful thinking.

## GORY DETAIL

THERE AREN'T AS MANY STORIES ABOUT OTHER HOUSEHOLD PETS SCAVENGING BODIES, BUT ONE HORRIFYING TALE INVOLVES A HAMSTER. A WOMAN WHO DIED OF PNEUMONIA WAS FOUND WITH STRANGE MARKS ON HER FACE. AS IT TURNS OUT, HER FREE-RANGE HAMSTER WAS USING BITS OF HER SKIN, FAT, AND TISSUE TO DECORATE ITS BURROW.

## YOU'RE NOT USING IT

Rats will also make a cozy home out of your body, but they have the courtesy to wait until you're mostly dried out before they then nest in your skeleton. They also "feather" their existing nests with hair and clothing from available corpses.

## THE GRIND

That doesn't mean they won't desecrate your corpse a tiny bit. Rodents gnaw on bones to get calcium and to grind down their front teeth, which never stop growing. And they're not fussy about who the bones belonged to.

## RETHINKING YOUR OPHIDIOPHOBIA

Despite their sometimes more frightful appearance, exotic pets like snakes and lizards want nothing to do with your dead body. They're also generally less likely to kill you in the first place than your furry friends.

"THE TROUBLE WITH THE RAT RACE IS THAT EVEN IF YOU WIN, YOU'RE STILL A RAT."

—LILY TOMLIN

# DYING IN WEIRD PLACES

## PRESERVED IN TIME AND SPACE

If you die in outer space, your body won't decompose because there's no oxygen to produce the necessary chemical reactions. If you happen to be floating near a heat source, your body will mummify. If not, it will freeze.

## THE FINAL FRONTIER

If you die in a space suit that still has oxygen, you will decompose, but only for as long as the oxygen flows. After that, see above.

## GORY DETAIL

THE FREEZING TEMPERATURES IN SPACE WON'T BE WHAT KILLS YOU. INSTEAD, YOUR BODY WILL SWELL AS THE WATER IN IT VAPORIZES, YOU'LL GET A NASTY SUNBURN FROM COSMIC RADIATION, AND THEN YOU'LL SUFFOCATE TO DEATH.

## ANTI-AGING HYDRATION

Bodies submerged in water decompose more slowly than those on land due to lower temperatures and oxygen levels. But once those bodies are removed from water, all bets are off, and decomp starts making up for lost time.

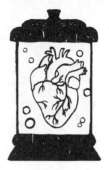

## FOR PEAT'S SAKE

European peat bogs, in particular, have been known to preserve bodies in astonishing detail for centuries thanks to low temps and oxygen combined with a highly acidic environment.

## · DUMB WAYS ᴛᴏ DIE ·

In a stunt intended (somehow) to raise awareness about the homeless, Robert Overacker decided to combine a jet ski with an improvised rocket booster and shoot himself over Niagara Falls. As if that weren't stupid enough, he forgot to secure his parachute. It floated away as he plunged to his death.

# PLAYING IT COOL

### HYPOTHERMIA IS HELPFUL

Medical professionals say, "You're not dead until you're warm and dead." That's because people can be brought back from the brink of freezing to death when warmed up. But if they reach 98.6°F with no signs of life, they're *dead* dead.

### PRESSING PAUSE ON DECOMP

There are two kinds of morgue freezers: positive and negative. The milder temps of positive freezers (35.6° to 39.2°F) can slow decomp, but the colder temps of negative freezers (5° to -13°F) can stop it in its tracks, allowing for long-term storage of bodies.

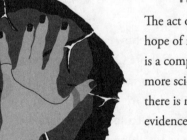

### THE DEEP FREEZE

The act of freezing a dead body in the hope of resuscitating it in the future is a complicated process that is still more sci-fi than science—specifically, there is not a shred of scientific evidence that it could ever work.

## ETERNAL OPTIMISTS

Roughly 300 optimistic Americans have had their bodies frozen in liquid nitrogen in case science discovers how to bring them back to life. And they pay around $28,000 for the pleasure.

........

## JUST TO CLARIFY

People have been getting this wrong for decades: The process of freezing a cadaver is called *cryonics*. The science of engineering super-low temperatures is *cryogenics*. The distinction's probably pretty important to the scientists who have nothing to do with dead bodies and would rather avoid any unfortunate mix-ups.

........

## ELSA WOULD NEVER

Despite some incredibly persistent rumors (or maybe propaganda for cryonics), Walt Disney did *not* have any part of himself frozen in the hopes of a scientific breakthrough.

"WHEN I DIE, I'M LEAVING MY BODY TO SCIENCE FICTION."
—STEVEN WRIGHT

# CHAPTER 2

# A Brief History of Death

IS HISTORY TEEMING WITH MORBID CURIOSITIES, BARBARIC RITUALS, AND DEADLY EVENTS? YES. IS IT ALSO CHOCK-FULL OF ODD CUSTOMS AND DEEPLY HELD BELIEFS THAT REFLECT THE BEST WISDOM—OR TOTAL FOLLY—OF THE TIMES? ABSOLUTELY. FROM MACABRE VICTORIAN STILL LIFES (STILL DEADS?) TO WORLD-CHANGING PLAGUES, THIS CHAPTER RUNS THE GRUESOME GAMUT.

# WHAT'S IN A NAME?

### EVERYONE HAS A THING

A taphophile is a person with a passion for all things funereal, including cemeteries, historical deaths, epitaphs, and gravestone rubbing. Other fun names for these peculiar folks are tombstone tourist, cemetery enthusiast, cemetery tourist, grave hunter, and graver. (If you're reading this, odds of you being a taphophile are pretty good.)

### THE FIRST WORD

The first recorded use of the word "funeral" was in Geoffrey Chaucer's *The Knight's Tale* in 1386. It's one of the few words you can actually make out in the original Middle English.

### A COMFORTING THOUGHT

The word "cemetery" comes from the Greek word *koimeterion*, which means "sleeping place" or "dormitory." The ancient Greeks believed that the dead were not gone, but only sleeping until they were resurrected.

## DEADLY TURNS OF PHRASE

There have been a lot of creative euphemisms for death over the years, including yield the crow a pudding (1599), slip one's wind (1772), hop the twig (1797), stick one's spoon in the wall (1873), snuff one's glim (1900), and climb the six-foot ladder (1950).

## PUSHING DAISIES

The particularly delightful and evocative saying "pushing up daisies" comes from nineteenth-century England. It cropped up a lot between soldiers during World War I and was even used in a 1918 poem by Wilfred Owen. (*Pushing Daisies* was also a morbidly dark TV show cut down in its prime in 2009.)

## · DUMB WAYS ᴛᴏ DIE ·

In 1751, renowned French physician and philosopher Julien Offray de La Mettrie died shortly after overindulging in pheasant pâté at a feast thrown in his honor. His fellow philosophers—never missing an opportunity to be morally superior—used him as a cautionary tale against materialism. But it's more than likely he died of food poisoning (because refrigeration wasn't invented until the 1800s).

# Good Grief

## GRIEF SPANS SPECIES

Grief rituals aren't specific to humans. Cetaceans (whales, dolphins, and porpoises) and primates (chimpanzees, gorillas, and Japanese macaques) have all been seen caring for their dead, particularly carrying around the bodies of babies for days or even weeks.

## AN ELEPHANT'S MEMORY

Elephants are well known for their emotional intelligence (they are associated with wisdom, after all). They'll visit their dead brethren for months—sometimes years—even standing over the bones. The 2003 death of elder matriarch Eleanor at the Samburu National Reserve in Kenya saw five different elephant families pay their respects.

## THE TINIEST UNDERTAKERS

Even bees, termites, and ants cart off their dead in a behavior called necrophoresis, but that may have more to do with preventing the spread of disease. Ants, in particular, appoint special undertakers whose job it is to bury or entomb the dead in a dedicated grave.

"MY WALLPAPER AND I ARE FIGHTING A DUEL TO THE DEATH. ONE OR THE OTHER OF US HAS GOT TO GO."

—OSCAR WILDE'S LAST WORDS

## A MORATORIUM ON MOURNING

Ancient China had rules for how long you were allowed to mourn the death of a child. Children under seven weren't given a funeral, and the parents of children who died under three months old were only allowed to cry one day for every month their child was alive.

........

## FELINE FINE

The Egyptian love for cats is well documented, so it should come as no surprise
that Egyptians took it hard when a favorite
feline died. The cat's owner would shave
their eyebrows to demonstrate their grief and
would mourn until they grew back.

## GORY DETAIL

IT WAS TOTALLY NORMAL IN THE 1800s TO CREATE
AND WEAR JEWELRY CONTAINING THE HAIR, TEETH, OR
ASHES OF DECEASED LOVED ONES, AS WELL AS TO TAKE
PHOTOS WITH YOUR DEAD RELATIVES AND DISPLAY
THE PICTURES. SMILE AND SAY, "GRAVE WAX!"

## STOPPING THE CLOCK

Victorians had a slew of characteristically dramatic postmortem rituals, including stopping clocks, closing curtains, and flipping portraits of the deceased.

## IT'S ONLY PROPER

Victorians were nothing if not stringent about etiquette—especially when it came to women. A widower was supposed to mourn for three months while a widow was stuck wearing black and lamenting the death of her husband for two and a half years (whether or not she actually liked him).

## · DUMB WAYS TO DIE ·

The Victorian sense of honor was so strict that, in 1892, a party of sailors let one of their own drown after he'd fallen overboard. The reason? They didn't want to offend the delicate sensibilities of the women on a nearby boat by stripping off their cumbersome clothing to dive in after him. By the time they came to their senses, it was too late.

# Finding Common Ground

### INTENTIONALLY GRAVE

Evidence suggests that the Neanderthals were the first human species to intentionally bury their dead, usually in family plots by their homes. (Considering that ants do this instinctually, that doesn't say much for human beings.)

### NOMADS NO MORE

The world's oldest known cemetery is the Gross Fredenwalde cemetery in Germany. It was discovered in 1962, a good 8,500 years after its use. And while the existence of a really old cemetery doesn't seem odd, it is, because the hunter-gatherers buried in it would have been nomadic, never staying in one place long enough to establish a graveyard.

### DYING LARGE

Wadi-us-Salaam in Iraq is said to be the largest cemetery in the world. It covers an area of 1,485.5 acres—making up nearly 30 percent of the city of Najaf—and contains around 6 million graves. It is also one of the oldest cemeteries in the world, dating back to the seventh century.

# GORY DETAIL

IF YOU'VE EVER TOURED A HISTORIC CHURCH, ODDS ARE GOOD THAT YOU'VE WALKED ON DEAD BODIES. IT WAS COMMON FOR PEOPLE (MOSTLY CLERGY AND UPPER CLASS) TO BE BURIED IN CRYPTS BELOW THE CHURCH (LIKE IN ST. PATRICK'S CATHEDRAL IN NEW YORK CITY) OR EVEN JUST BENEATH THE FLOORBOARDS (LIKE IN LONDON'S WESTMINSTER ABBEY).

## HGTV DREAM CRYPT

The 500-year-old stone floors of England's Bath Abbey nearly gave out because of the 6,000 bodies stuffed (rather unceremoniously, for a church) beneath them. They had to dig everyone up, fill the voids left by decomposing corpses, and replace more than 2,000 original stones.

## DEAD WEIGHT

The Middle Ages saw the creation of so-called corpse roads to transport the dead from remote areas to parishes for burial. But no one wanted rotting corpses traipsing through the main streets, so these roads wound through pastures and over hills. Because carrying a body was just too easy.

## DEATH, BUT MAKE IT PRETTY

We have the Victorians to thank for the orderly, garden-like graveyards we know and fill today, which tracks with their love of a neat hedge and mown grass (not to mention the era's high body count, which necessitated country cemeteries).

## A BREATH OF FRESH AIR

Unlike a lot of Victorian England, these organized graveyards weren't just for appearance's sake. At the time, the medical community believed in miasma theory—essentially, they thought disease was spread by breathing air infused with the essence of rotting corpses, among other noxious things.

### · DUMB WAYS TO DIE ·

In 1872, pallbearer Henry Taylor stumbled and fell in London's Kensal Green Cemetery mid-carry. He wasn't the only one to fall down on the job, though—the other pallbearers accidentally let go of the coffin, which landed on poor Henry and killed him.

# DEATH WITH A SIDE OF TUNNEL VISION

### PRACTICALLY THE SAME

The Roman catacombs were utilized by early Christians who believed they would need their bodies for resurrection but couldn't afford the fancy above-ground tombs that sit along the same road, the Appian Way. It's like renting an apartment—if you know you're moving, you can do without the bells and whistles.

### WHEN IN ROME

The Christians weren't the first inhabitants of the Roman catacombs, though. They served as a pagan burial site before early Jewish inhabitants of Rome began using them between 11 BC and 5 CE. But with more than twelve miles of tunnels, there was room enough for everyone.

### NOT SHORT ON IDEAS

Napoléon, in his quest for power and status in Europe, decided to copy the Italians and give the public access to Paris's Catacombs. Because the previous workers had unceremoniously tossed the bones into heaps, he had his men stack them all nice and pretty for the tourists. To this day, you can visit them while munching on a croissant.

## GORY DETAIL

DURING THE EIGHTEENTH CENTURY, PARIS'S BODIES WERE
PILING UP IN THE CITY'S OVERBURDENED CEMETERIES. NOT ONLY
DID THE DECOMPOSING BODIES LYING AROUND EVERYWHERE
MAKE THE CITY STINK, THEY ALSO FUELED THE SPREAD OF
DISEASE. SO, IN 1785, NIGHTTIME FUNERAL PROCESSIONS
BEGAN CARTING BODIES FROM CEMETERIES TO THE CITY'S
UNDERGROUND LIMESTONE QUARRIES (AKA THE CATACOMBS),
WHILE PRIESTS FOLLOWED ALONG TO BLESS THEM.

## DON'T MIND THE GAPS

With six million skeletons in one sprawling underground Parisian labyrinth, it's hard to keep track when things go missing. And go missing they do—especially the skulls. So, if you visit and notice an odd hole here and there, know that someone somewhere took home a really gross souvenir.

## GO DOWN IN HISTORY

The award for largest system of catacombs in the world goes to Odessa, Ukraine. The 1,500 miles of limestone tunnels date back to at least the seventeenth century and hid Soviet rebels during World War I and smugglers during the Cold War.

"WHAT
THE DEVIL
DO YOU MEAN
TO SING TO ME,
PRIEST? YOU ARE
OUT OF TUNE."

—COMPOSER
JEAN-PHILIPPE RAMEAU'S
LAST WORDS

## SKULLS SEND A MESSAGE

In Serbia, you can visit a tower made with the skulls of Serbian rebels who, rather than surrendering to the Turkish Ottomans, shot at their own gunpowder reserves and blew up both sides. A Turkish commander who avoided the fray built the tower as a warning to other rebels.

........

## LIKE FINE WINE

As if catacombs themselves weren't eerie enough, Italy's Catacombe dei Cappuccini adds another layer of creepiness. A naturally occurring preservative in the catacombs mummified the dead, making them look like they're just sleeping in their Sunday best.

## · DUMB WAYS TO DIE ·

In 1783, Philibert Aspairt went looking for alcohol that he knew was stored in the Paris catacombs and died just ten feet from an exit—liquor bottle in hand—after getting lost. You can't entirely blame him, though. Back then, they only had candlelight and their wits to guide them. And since he'd found the liquor, he probably didn't have his wits.

# NECESSITY IS THE MOTHER OF INVENTION

### PINE BOX NO MORE

There's a difference between a coffin and a casket. Coffins are the old-fashioned options, made of wood, tapered at the feet, and best known for housing vampires. Caskets are the newer creations and are lined, rectangular, and as expensive as a down payment on a new car.

### THE LAST BASTION

Coffins went out of style in the late 1800s in favor of the fancier, more fortress-like caskets we see today due to changing attitudes about death. (Namely, that no one wants to think about being eaten by worms.)

### CRAFTED FOR ETERNITY

The first documented use of burial vaults dates back to the late 1800s. They used to be made of wood or brick, but today they're more likely to be made of metal, concrete, and—of course—plastic.

# GORY DETAIL

LACK OF MEDICAL KNOW-HOW WASN'T THE ONLY FATAL ISSUE BACK IN THE DAY—SANITATION WAS THE STUFF OF NIGHTMARES BEFORE THE ADOPTION OF SEWER SYSTEMS IN THE MID-NINETEENTH CENTURY. PEOPLE HAD ZERO COMPREHENSION OF BACTERIA, BARELY BATHED, AND TOSSED THE CONTENTS OF THEIR CHAMBER POTS AND PRIVIES INTO LOCAL WATERWAYS.

## KNOW WHEN TO FOLD 'EM

The first folding chair may have been invented by a mortician. Sick of putting out heavy chairs for every funeral, Seth G. Tufts created his "Undertaker's Chair" in the mid-1800s. He wasn't the first to patent it, but an original picture of his creation remains in the Tufts Schildmeyer Family Funeral Home.

## AN HEIR AND A SPARE (OR SPARES)

Before the advent of modern medicine, as many as 40 percent of children didn't reach adulthood. That's why eighteenth-century graveyards are filled with tiny, cherub-marked graves. And maybe why families were so large—you needed spares.

# NOT QUITE DEAD YET

## SAVED BY THE BELL

The phrase "saved by the bell" doesn't actually come from the nineteenth-century practice of attaching bells to coffins in case the occupant was buried alive. It refers to a boxer saved from losing the round. Even so, the fear of being buried alive (taphephobia) was completely justified pre-twentieth century.

## GRAVE CONCERN

After being scarred for life by seeing a young girl almost buried alive, Count Michel de Karnice-Karnicki created a safety coffin in 1896. A glass ball dangling over the dead (or not-dead) would stir with any movement, open a hatch, and set off a bell. But the overly sensitive invention didn't account for the body's expansion during decomposition, so it never caught on.

## GORY DETAIL

JUST A FEW OF THE WAYS PEOPLE ENSURED THAT SOMEONE WAS REALLY DEAD BEFORE ADVANCES IN MEDICAL SCIENCE AND COMMON SENSE INCLUDE: SHOVING NEEDLES INTO SENSITIVE AREAS, BURNING THEM WITH RED-HOT POKERS, AND CHOPPING OFF FINGERS, IF NOT ENTIRE HANDS.

## BLOWING SMOKE

Drowning victims were sometimes given smoke enemas to see if being warmed up from the inside would help them breathe again. This is where the phrase "blowing smoke up your ass" comes from.

## NO VAMPIRES ALLOWED

Although we joke about zombie apocalypses today, people in the olden days genuinely feared the dead—especially vampires—rising up. To prevent this from happening, they took many precautions, including driving iron stakes through the bodies, burying the dead under bricks, placing scythes over their necks, binding them in chains and ropes, and even nailing their jaws shut.

## FACE DOWN IN THE DIRT

In the Middle Ages, people believed that vampires could bite their way out of the grave, so they buried suspected vampires face down. Better safe than drained of all your blood.

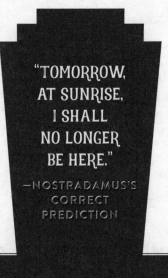

"TOMORROW,
AT SUNRISE,
I SHALL
NO LONGER
BE HERE."

—NOSTRADAMUS'S
CORRECT
PREDICTION

## ON THE BRIGHT SIDE

Although many who were mistakenly pronounced dead ended up that way anyway once they were buried, a few got lucky. Sixteenth-century Englishman Matthew Wall lived twenty-four more years after his coffin was dropped by pallbearers navigating slippery terrain, jostling him awake just in time.

## THE ODDS ARE IN YOUR FAVOR

Not only do doctors perform a battery of diagnostics to confirm death nowadays, but thanks to modern refrigeration and preservation techniques (like embalming), there isn't such a rush to get soon-to-be-rotting bodies into the ground. That makes your odds of being buried alive closer to nil—but never zero.

## · DUMB WAYS TO DIE ·

Two different women in their forties were buried alive in Peraia, Greece, in 2014. Both were discovered newly dead after mourners heard screaming coming from their burial sites—one died from asphyxia, the other from a heart attack, understandably. (If you're sick, it might be worth avoiding Peraia.)

# INVASION OF THE BODY SNATCHERS

### ONE FOOT IN THE GRAVE

Body snatching (stealing corpses from graves) was a real problem during the boom of medical schools in the Civil War era, and the deathcare industry got creative. They buried people in everything from locking cast-iron caskets to "casket torpedoes"—devices that were like small shotguns filled with explosives and would fire if anyone disturbed the body.

### A NEW KIND OF RIB CAGE

Iron cages surrounding the buried were thought by some to keep the dead from rising. But newer theories suggest that the cages—called mortsafes—protected the dead from these so-called "resurrection men" (aka grave robbers).

### THOSE MEDDLING KIDS

People weren't just digging up bodies to sell to medical schools—they were also "manufacturing" their own. Scottish body snatchers William Burke and William Hare murdered fifteen people and sold their corpses to medical schools for dissection before being turned in by nosy neighbors.

## HOW WOULD THEY KNOW?

Body harvesting and grave robbing were such a problem in San Francisco's overburdened Yerba Bueno Cemetery during the gold rush that the city set out to rebury the bodies elsewhere. But when they ran out of money, they just quietly sealed up about 50,000 graves and built city landmarks like UN Plaza and City Hall overtop.

## NOTHING TO SEE HERE

Police generally did nothing to stop grave robbers. They considered body harvesting a victimless crime because the deceased could no longer claim ownership of their body.

## GORY DETAIL

GRAVE ROBBERS WOULD DIG AT THE HEAD OF THE GRAVE, BREAK OPEN THE COFFIN, SLIP THE BODY OUT BY A HOOK, AND TRANSPORT IT IN A WHISKEY BARREL TO MASK THE SMELL. POSSIBLY WORST OF ALL (THOUGH IT'S A SLIDING SCALE), THE MEDICAL SCHOOL THAT BOUGHT THE CORPSE WOULD THEN SELL THE "ROTGUT" WHISKEY. HENCE THE TERM "STIFF DRINK."

## NOT IN MY JOB DESCRIPTION

Even renowned medical school Johns Hopkins quietly kept a grave robber on staff to help supply them with fresh bodies for dissection in its early days. Or, rather, they just added body-harvesting duties to janitor William "King Bill" Hartley's job description.

·········

## IT'S CALLED PROGRESS

The lovely period in history riddled with body snatching didn't end because the snatchers grew a conscience. From the mid-1800s to early 1900s, new anatomy laws were enacted by individual states, giving medical schools free rein to take possession of the bodies of the poor, which put a damper on the black market for cadavers.

## · DUMB WAYS ₸ DIE ·

Life was obviously tougher in the late 1800s. For example, there were no alarm clocks. So, in 1886, lamplighter Samuel Wardell invented his own. It involved a clock, a shelf, and a weight that would fall at the predetermined time. Tipsy one Christmas night, Wardell misjudged the measurements and sent the weight crashing down on his head in the morning.

# LET IT BURN

## BODY REQUIRED

Cremation dates back to the Stone Age, but burial rose in popularity with the Christian belief that a body—regardless of its condition—was necessary for resurrection on Judgment Day.

## IF YOU BUILD IT

Despite cremation's ancient roots, crematories didn't pop up in the United States until the late 1800s. Dr. Francis Julius LeMoyne built the first one in Washington, Pennsylvania, in 1876.

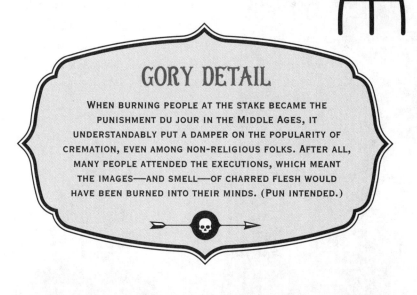

## GORY DETAIL

When burning people at the stake became the punishment du jour in the Middle Ages, it understandably put a damper on the popularity of cremation, even among non-religious folks. After all, many people attended the executions, which meant the images—and smell—of charred flesh would have been burned into their minds. (Pun intended.)

## UP FOR INTERPRETATION

Despite many Christian beliefs surrounding burial, the Bible doesn't actually give any specifics on final-disposition requirements. In fact, it speaks pretty genially about both burial and cremation. So any staunch beliefs one way or the other are the result of individual interpretation.

## TO EACH THEIR OWN

Religions span the spectrum on the subject of cremation. Islam and Judaism forbid it while Buddhism prefers it, and Hinduism requires it. Catholicism ended a ban on it in 1963 but still frowns upon spreading ashes.

## GET THE WOOD

The use of funeral pyres isn't relegated to the Vikings or ancient Rome—this method of cremation is still used in largely Hindu countries such as India and Nepal today. And although they're rare in the Western world, they're not unheard of.

"TURN ME OVER.
I'M DONE
ON THIS SIDE."

—ST. LAWRENCE,
WHILE BEING
BURNED ALIVE
IN ROME

# WAKING THE DEAD

### TRANSITION ASSISTANCE

Far from the canapé-laden gatherings of today, wakes were originally prayer-infused vigils believed to help the dead transition from one plane to the next (and keep evil spirits from snatching the body). And they were traditionally held in the family home.

. . . . . . . .

### AT DEATH'S DOOR

The terms "coffin door" and "funeral doors" have been making the rounds for about a century. They refer to an outside door to the parlor or double doors from the entryway to the parlor, both meant to squeeze a casket into a home for viewing. (That might be a shocking revelation to a few owners of what they thought were French doors.)

. . . . . . . .

### THE BODYGUARD

Judaic tradition requires burials to take place within twenty-four hours, which is good because it also requires someone to keep watch over the body until it's in the ground in a ritual called shemira. Thankfully, the mourners can work in shifts.

## AN HERB WITH PURPOSE

Rosemary was the preferred plant for funerals in ancient Egypt and Rome, not only for its pleasant aroma but also because the evergreen plant symbolizes remembrance and eternal life.

.........

## PUT ON
## YOUR DRESS TOGA

Speaking of the Romans, they were the first to don black when in mourning. (You didn't even know togas came in colors other than white, did you?) The Brits, and Victorians in particular, helped make the habit stick.

### GORY DETAIL

FLOWERS AND CANDLES AREN'T FUNERAL STAPLES BECAUSE OF THEIR VISUAL APPEAL OR SYMBOLISM. IN THE CENTURIES BEFORE MODERN PRESERVATION TECHNIQUES, THEY WERE USED TO MASK UNPLEASANT ODORS.

# LET'S GET THIS PARTY STARTED

### PARTY POOPERS

Colonial legislators had to put a legal stop to increasingly extravagant funerals because keeping up with the dead Joneses was bankrupting widows. To keep the parties modest, they put a cap on pricing and fined anyone who brought liquor.

........

### AN IRISH GOODBYE

In many cultures, wakes and funerals are treated like celebrations rather than sober affairs. In fact, there may not be anything sober about them. Irish wakes, for example, often result in mourners drinking, singing, telling jokes and stories, and even playing pranks.

..........

### DON'T FORGET THE TAMALES

Día de los Muertos, which originated with indigenous communities in Mexico, is like a festive family reunion for the dead and the living. Those who still have a pulse fill brightly colored altars with offerings like carnations and favorite foods for the ones who don't to enjoy.

## YOU STILL HAVE TO EAT

Food is a universal language at funerals. While "widower casserole" and veggie trays are popular among Americans, Victorians had funeral biscuits, Mexicans have traditionally enjoyed *pan de muerto* (literally "bread of the dead"), and Italians bake cookies that represent the bones of dead saints (*ossa dei morti*).

## LAISSEZ LES BON TEMPS ROULER

New Orleans, Louisiana, has some famously fun funerals. Since the 1800s, mourners and strangers alike have danced through the streets in the wake of a jazz band playing upbeat tunes to honor the dead and celebrate the joy of life in what they call the "second line" parade.

## · DUMB WAYS TO DIE ·

Celebrations have always come with risks. On average, twenty-four people per year are killed by wayward champagne corks. When you hear that "pop" at a restaurant, party, or even a funeral, duck and cover!

## A HEALTHY RELATIONSHIP WITH THE DEAD

In Indonesia, the Toraja people practice a ritual called Ma'nene, "the ceremony of cleaning corpses." Every three years, they exhume the bodies of their beloved ancestors, wash them, dress them in new clothes, and parade them around the village. Westerners might balk, but it's a really well-adjusted stance on death.

........

## NOTHING LIKE A FRESH SHROUD

Madagascans also dig up their dead relatives in a celebration called Famadihana, or "turning of the bones," every five to seven years. But they don't parade them around. They just sing and dance with the decomposing bodies at the burial site before covering them again with new shrouds.

........

## A CLEAN SWEEP

For 2,500 years, Chinese people have celebrated the Qingming Festival by showing up to their ancestors' graves with food and willow trees (or just branches) to celebrate the dead, ward off evil spirits, and generally tidy up the place.

"NOW IS NOT THE TIME FOR MAKING NEW ENEMIES."

—VOLTAIRE'S LAST WORDS TO A PRIEST ASKING HIM TO RENOUNCE SATAN

# Making a Name for Yourself

## WHEN DEAD IN ROME

Obits, like many things, started with the Romans around 59 BC, but they weren't the flowery or informative odes we're used to today. They were simple death announcements printed next to the day's news in the *Acta Diurna* ("Daily Events"), a papyrus newsletter.

--------

## VIPS ONLY

The average Joe didn't get an obituary until the twentieth century. Earlier than that, written homages to the deceased were generally reserved for prominent (read: wealthy) figures.

## · DUMB WAYS TO DIE ·

Jamaican political activist Marcus Garvey, Jr. died after reading his own obituary in 1940. To be fair, he'd already had a stroke and was in unstable health, so his death wasn't entirely due to the premature obituary planted by his political rivals. But it certainly didn't help.

# A Religious Experience

## SOUNDS LIKE A PERSONAL PROBLEM

In the early days of Christianity, religion had little to do with death or burial. Dying was considered a private matter for immediate family to deal with. Even doctors washed their hands of hopeless cases without worrying about declaring them dead, while religious figures focused on general worship.

·········

## BLAME THE PAGANS

The frivolity of Irish wakes didn't sit well with the Catholic Church, which tried to put an end to the alcohol-infused custom (especially because Protestant reformers were looking down their noses at the Catholics for it). But the tradition's pagan roots were too strong.

## GORY DETAIL

TIBETAN BUDDHISTS PRACTICE WHAT THEY PREACH—NAMELY NON-ATTACHMENT—BY SKIPPING THE BURIAL AND LEAVING THE CHOPPED-UP BODIES OF THEIR DEAD ON MOUNTAINTOPS FOR VULTURES AND OTHER CREATURES TO FEAST ON. THE PRACTICE IS CALLED SKY BURIAL, OR CELESTIAL BURIAL.

# BEST OF LUCK TO YOU

## THE ULTIMATE JINX

In some areas of the world, including Japan and Korea, it's long been considered bad luck to say the words "death" or "funeral" to the living. Many people even avoid saying the word "four" in China because it sounds like the word for "death." There's a word for this fear of four: tetraphobia.

## TWO FEET OUT THE DOOR

According to the principles of feng shui, sleeping with your feet facing the door is thought to tempt fate because, when you die, you'll be leaving the room feet first. You don't want to make it too easy on the Grim Reaper!

## FINAL NAIL IN THE COFFIN

Coffin nails have a long history of warding off bad luck or bringing it, depending on the user's intent and actions. For example, you could wear one as a ring or keep one in your pocket for protection against evil spirits. They were also believed to cure rheumatism, childhood illness, and warts. However, some people believed that hammering a coffin nail into someone's footprint would make that person fall ill.

## THERE'S NO CRYING IN BALI

The Balinese keep the mourning and tearfulness to a minimum, particularly because they believe that tears falling on a body can cause all sorts of problems, from the dead ending up in a room with a partially obstructed view in heaven to malevolent spirits pestering them for eternity.

## DOGS ARE GOOD LUCK

In Zoroastrianism, the ancient religion of modern-day Iran, funeral rites included cleansing the body in unconsecrated bull's urine and letting a sacred dog visit it twice to banish evil spirits before giving it a sky burial (aka leaving it to be eaten by vultures).

## · DUMB WAYS TO DIE ·

In 1871, lawyer Clement Vallandigham shot himself in the stomach while attempting to demonstrate his client's innocence in a murder trial. His defense: that the victim accidentally shot himself during a barroom brawl. Talk about tempting fate—but Vallandigham didn't pull the trigger. His clothing did, when the gun's trigger snagged inside his pocket. On the bright side, he won his case.

# Apparently, You Can Take It with You

### EVERYTHING BUT THE KITCHEN SINK

These days, it's not unusual to tuck Uncle Jack's prized baseball card into his casket. But the belief that life goes on after death made some ancient civilizations pack graves like moving trucks. Vikings could be buried with whole ships while noble Egyptians were sometimes interred with live—and incredibly unlucky—servants and animals.

........

### A GRIMM TAKE ON SELF-HELP

*Beetlejuice*'s *Handbook for the Recently Deceased* isn't entirely fictional. The Egyptians created their *Book of the Dead* somewhere between 1550 and

1070 BCE. Instead of being just another tourist's guide to the other side, though, it included hundreds of spells to help the newly dead navigate the afterlife.

........

### THE WORK NEVER ENDS

Ancient Egyptians believed that the afterlife was a mirror image of life on earth—back-breaking workload and all. In an attempt to rest in peace, they were buried with "shabti" dolls, which were inscribed with spells allowing the dolls to spring to life on the other side and step in for the dead when the god Osiris eventually called them to duty.

## A PENNY FOR YOUR ROT

The tradition of placing coins on the eyes of the dead started with the ancient Greeks, who believed the deceased needed the loose change to pay the ferryman, Charon, to help them cross the River Styx to the underworld. Later cultures continued to do it mostly as a cheap and easy way to keep the decedent's rotting eyes closed.

## YOGI BEAR WOULD BE THRILLED

Egyptians weren't just buried with household goods and reading materials. They were also sent on their final journey with a veritable picnic basket of bread, fruits, and vegetables, some of which was itself mummified to help keep it from spoiling.

## GORY DETAIL

SATI WAS AN ANCIENT HINDU CUSTOM IN WHICH A DECEASED MAN'S WIDOW WAS BURNED ALIVE ON HIS FUNERAL PYRE—WHETHER OR NOT SHE WAS WILLING. THE NAME IRONICALLY COMES FROM THE HINDU GODDESS OF MARITAL FELICITY AND LONGEVITY.

# PRESERVATION IS VITAL TO HISTORY

### IT WORKS FOR FRUIT

Ancient Egyptians are credited with the genesis of embalming practices (more on that later), but plenty of other cultures practiced some version of it. Babylonians, Persians, and Syrians preserved their dead by placing them in jars of honey, like human peaches.

### SO MANY BODIES, SO LITTLE TIME

Embalming became popular in America during the Civil War, when dead bodies were easy to come by but had to be shipped home in one piece (or as many pieces as were available) for burial because no one wanted to be left on enemy soil.

### NOT-SO-HONORABLE DISCHARGE

Embalmers advertised their services by embalming unidentified soldiers and sticking them outside their tents at attention. As the death rates increased, so did the entrepreneurial surgeons' fees.

"THEY COULDN'T HIT AN ELEPHANT AT THIS DIST—"

—UNION GENERAL JOHN SEDGWICK, WHO WAS MIDSENTENCE WHEN SHOT AND KILLED

## SOME MUCH-NEEDED RED TAPE

Embalmers' practice of price gouging became so rampant that the War Department had to step in. They issued Order 39, which forced embalmers to earn a license and use set pricing guidelines. This marks the first time the government attempted to regulate the deathcare industry, but certainly not the last.

## NO REST FOR THE WEARY

Abraham Lincoln couldn't even rest when he was dead. His body was embalmed so it could travel the country on a morbid tour to score political support for unification.

## · DUMB WAYS TO DIE ·

In 1919, a giant vat of molasses exploded and unleashed a 40-foot wave of the sticky stuff into the streets of Boston, killing twenty-one people (and more than a few animals) and injuring 150 more. Some were stuck in the molasses itself, some were hit by debris and hurtling rivets, and some were hurled into the harbor by the force of the thing.

# All Wrapped Up

## BETTER THAN A SEAWEED WRAP

Modern spa days have nothing on ancient Egyptian embalming sessions. The mummification process—which was pricey and therefore mostly exclusive to wealthy Egyptians—could last as many as seventy days and involve a number of priests to get things just right.

## MASK UP

The priests doing the bulk of the prep work had to act as both religious official and embalmer. And, like any good morgue employee, they wore a mask: the mask of Anubis, the jackal-headed god of the dead.

## GORY DETAIL

THE FIRST THING ANY GOOD JACKAL-FACED PRIEST WOULD DO WAS PULL THE DEAD GUY'S BRAINS OUT THROUGH HIS NOSE USING A LONG HOOK. BECAUSE THE BRAIN WAS CONSIDERED A USELESS ORGAN, THEY TOSSED THE TORN-UP BITS OF IT OUT WITH THE TRASH.

## LIKE CREEPY PRESERVES

Next, they would remove the deceased's liver, lungs, stomach, and intestines (the old-fashioned way, through a cut in their stomach). But these weren't tossed on the trash heap with the brain. Instead, they were placed in special containers, called canopic jars, that were guarded by protective deities.

..........

## SOULMATES

Because Egyptians believed you'd need your body in the afterlife, the goal of mummification was to perfectly preserve it so the soul could recognize, re-enter, and use it. After a few tries, they realized how quickly organs decay—hence the jars.

..........

## THE HEART OF THE MATTER

The Egyptians believed the heart was the essence of a person and the true source of intelligence and emotion, so it was the one organ that got to stay put during the mummification process.

## SALT OF THE EARTH

To keep the body in pristine postmortem condition, the priests used salt to suck all of the moisture out of it. They'd cover and fill the body with natron for forty days. Then they'd give it a little rinse and fill any unsightly sunken areas with linen.

## TOMB STAGING

While the priests were busy salting and wrapping the body like a lunch special, workers were busy prepping the tomb with art, food, spells, and personal belongings like they were staging a home for an HGTV renovation show.

## GORY DETAIL

THE FACT THAT CATS WERE REVERED IN ANCIENT EGYPT MAY HAVE GOTTEN MORE THAN A FEW OF THEM KILLED AND MUMMIFIED AS SACRIFICES TO THE GODS. HISTORIANS BELIEVE SOME FARMERS EVEN BRED THEM FOR THIS PURPOSE. ONE TOMB DISCOVERED IN 1888 HELD HUNDREDS OF THOUSANDS OF THE PRESERVED CREATURES.

## THE LITTLE DETAILS

Every finger and toe got wrapped with linen before the whole hand and foot (and the rest of the body), using up hundreds of yards of fabric that the priests sprinkled with amulets and spells for protection.

........

## AN UNDERSTANDABLE MIXUP

We have far fewer mummies to study today because Europeans went through a phase of grinding them up and eating them to cure a variety of ailments. And it was all because of a misunderstanding. After all, "mumia" (the Persian healing herb) does sound an awful lot like "mummy."

........

## NO RESPECT FOR THE DEAD

That's not the only thing mummies were used for. Traveling to Egypt and bringing home gruesome souvenirs to display in your home was a favorite pastime of the upper class in the nineteenth century. It wasn't uncommon (however morally repugnant) to find mummified hands, feet, and even heads being used as decor.

"SHE STILL FASCINATES ME."
—RICHARD BURTON'S DYING WORDS ABOUT ELIZABETH TAYLOR

## THE ORIGIN OF UNBOXING VIDEOS?

In a similar vein (vain?), Victorians were known to throw
the occasional "mummy unwrapping" party. It started
with former circus performer Giovanni Belzoni putting on
a show of Egyptian antiquities and unwrapping one for a
fascinated crowd of 2,000 people near Piccadilly Circus.

## ARTISTIC LICENSE

Around the sixteenth century, artists started using a color called "mummy
brown" in their work, but not everyone realized the pigment was actually
ground-up mummy. Artist Edward Burne-Jones held a little funeral in his
garden for the paint when he found out.

# PRESERVED BY THE ELEMENTS

## BOGGED DOWN FOR AGES

The highly acidic water, low temperature, and a lack of oxygen in peat bogs has been known to preserve bodies for thousands of years. These naturally occurring mummies are delightfully called "bog bodies." One Iron Age man discovered in Denmark in 1950 was so perfectly preserved that people mistook him for a recent murder victim.

## HEADS-UP TO WOULD-BE CRIMINALS

Remember grave wax (that lovely corpse preservative made from body fat) from page 44? It can preserve bodies—and criminal evidence—for centuries. In 1913, authorities found the wax-covered bodies of the Higgins brothers in Scotland and were able to solve their two-year-old murder.

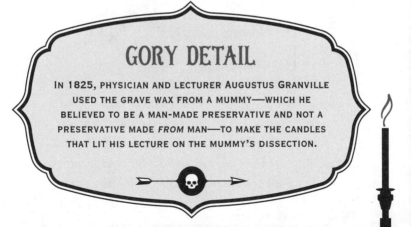

## GORY DETAIL

IN 1825, PHYSICIAN AND LECTURER AUGUSTUS GRANVILLE USED THE GRAVE WAX FROM A MUMMY—WHICH HE BELIEVED TO BE A MAN-MADE PRESERVATIVE AND NOT A PRESERVATIVE MADE *FROM* MAN—TO MAKE THE CANDLES THAT LIT HIS LECTURE ON THE MUMMY'S DISSECTION.

## MUMMY JUANITA

In 1995, archaeologists discovered a completely frozen and therefore perfectly preserved young Incan girl who was sacrificed to the gods atop a Peruvian mountain sometime in the mid-1400s. Mercifully, her cause of death was blunt-force trauma to the head, not freezing.

## TALK ABOUT GALLOWS HUMOR

Nederland, Colorado, celebrates the Frozen Dead Guy Days festival each year, using a more-than-century-old frozen corpse as a mascot. The honorary dead guy is Grandpa Bredo, a man kept on dry ice in a shed in a DIY cryonics setup. Celebrants can enjoy coffin racing, frozen salmon tossing, costumed polar plunging, and frozen T-shirt contests.

## · DUMB WAYS TO DIE ·

English philosopher and lawyer Francis Bacon died from pneumonia at a friend's house in 1626 after playing with a dead chicken in the snow and literally catching his death of cold. He had technically been studying the effects of weather on meat, but that doesn't make it any less strange.

# Drinking (Blood) to Your Health

## FORGET THE TYLENOL

Ancient Romans drank the blood of slain gladiators to absorb the vitality of the strong young men. But even well into the Renaissance, people believed that crushing and consuming parts of the dead could infuse them with the dead's spirit and cure what ailed them (e.g., a pulverized skull for a headache).

## A DASH OF COGNITIVE DISSONANCE

Europeans in the sixteenth century justified the subjugation of Native Americans through myths of tribal cannibalism while they, themselves, were drinking up tinctures made from dead friends and relatives.

## GORY DETAIL

THERE USED TO BE A DISTURBINGLY PERSISTENT PRACTICE OF TURNING TO CANNIBALISM AS MEDICINE. FOR EXAMPLE, PEOPLE USED TO PAY EXECUTIONERS FOR BLOOD IN THE SIXTEENTH AND SEVENTEENTH CENTURIES AND DRINK IT—FRESH AND WARM—AS A HEALTH TONIC.

## A KING'S RANSOM

A remedy called "the King's drops" made the rounds in the seventeenth century. It was made from human skulls soaked in alcohol and was said to be good for gout, edema, and "all fevers putrid or pestilential." Why was it called that? Supposedly, King Charles II of England paid £6,000 for the recipe.

## GRANDFATHER SOUP, ANYONE?

Several tribal cultures, like the Wari' of Brazil, used to engage in endo-cannibalism, or funerary cannibalism—in other words, eating the dead as a method of final disposition and a heartfelt expression of community. Suddenly, sky burials don't seem so startling, do they?

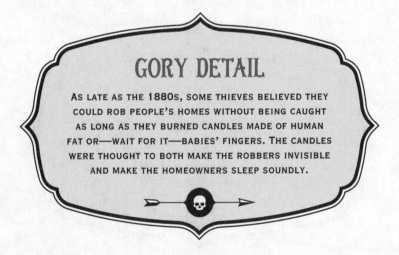

### GORY DETAIL

AS LATE AS THE 1880S, SOME THIEVES BELIEVED THEY COULD ROB PEOPLE'S HOMES WITHOUT BEING CAUGHT AS LONG AS THEY BURNED CANDLES MADE OF HUMAN FAT OR—WAIT FOR IT—BABIES' FINGERS. THE CANDLES WERE THOUGHT TO BOTH MAKE THE ROBBERS INVISIBLE AND MAKE THE HOMEOWNERS SLEEP SOUNDLY.

# A Plague on All the Houses

## PLAGUE BY NUMBERS

Historians are fuzzy on the numbers because records did not include rural populations, but the Black Death killed somewhere between 75 and 200 million people worldwide, including a good 30 to 50 percent of the European population, within just a few years.

## NO STEMMING THIS TIDE

The plague had already hit China, India, Persia, Syria, and Egypt when it came to Europe in 1347 aboard twelve ships that docked in Sicily, full of dead and soon-to-be-dead sailors. Authorities tried to turn the boats away, but it was too late.

## · DUMB WAYS TO DIE ·

London can't catch a break, death-wise. Eight people died in a beer tsunami in the streets near Tottenham Court Road when Horse Shoe Brewery's 22-foot-high wooden fermentation tank—which held over 3,500 barrels (320,000 gallons!) of brown porter ale—gave out. The event became known as the London Beer Flood of 1814, and it gave new meaning to "drowning your sorrows."

## SHARED TRAUMA TRUMPS GRIEF

Some experts have traced the West's attitude toward grief—which can best be described as "get over it already"—to the plague. With bodies dropping all around the place and no one wanting to tend to them for fear of the illness that felled them, funeral rites and mourning rituals got short shrift.

........

## JUSTICE FOR THE RATS

Rats got a bad rap for spreading the plague, but the true culprits were the fleas hitching a ride on the unsuspecting rodents.

........

## NO SHEEP TO SHEAR

The plague didn't infect just people and rats. Cows, goats, pigs, sheep, and chickens all fell victim. In fact, so many sheep died that it caused a wool shortage in Europe (which was, admittedly, the least of their problems).

"NEVER YET
HAS DEATH BEEN
FRIGHTENED AWAY
BY SCREAMING."

—TIMUR
THE CONQUEROR'S
LAST WORDS

## NOT AGAIN

The idea that graves should be six feet deep comes from a 1665 plague resurgence in England. The mayor of London—desperate to avoid repeating history—thought it might help limit the spread of disease. Of course, increased sanitation might have been a better policy change.

## BETTER LIVING THROUGH CHEMISTRY

The World Health Organization reports that there are still between 1,000 and 3,000 cases of the plague each year—even in the United States. Quick treatment with modern antibiotics (and much higher standards when it comes to sanitation) keeps it from decimating the population again.

# ANOTHER DAY, ANOTHER DEADLY EVENT

## SOMEONE SHOULD LOOK INTO THIS

Tuberculosis is one of those old-timey diseases that you think was relegated to the history books—the earliest mention of the disease was 3,000 years ago, and it accounted for 25 percent of all deaths between 1600 and 1800. But it also infected 10.6 million people and killed 1.6 million of them worldwide in 2021.

## SLANDERING THE MESSENGER

The famously deadly 1918 Spanish Flu that killed up to 40 percent of the world's population didn't actually originate in Spain. The since-maligned country was the first to report the illness because it was one of the few to remain neutral during World War I, allowing it to report news uncensored.

## THE BEGINNINGS OF BIOLOGICAL WARFARE

In at least one instance of total moral failure, colonists purposely tried to infect Native Americans with smallpox—a deadly disease that killed hundreds of millions of people before it was eradicated in 1977—by gifting them blankets infected with the virus.

## HAVE A COW

Cowpox, smallpox's less deadly cousin, is responsible for not only eradicating smallpox but also for modern vaccines. Dr. Edward Jenner discovered that being infected with cowpox made people immune to smallpox and developed the first vaccine in 1796. "Vaccine" even comes from the Latin word for cow (*vacca*).

## SIDE EFFECTS MAY INCLUDE CAPITALISM

Roughly 40 million people have died of HIV (human immunodeficiency virus), a disease that was claiming 50,000 American lives each year at its peak in 1995. Today, treatment is so effective and widely available that it's rivaled only by weight loss drugs in the onslaught of pharmaceutical ads.

## · DUMB WAYS ᴛᴏ DIE ·

A startling number of famous composers died of syphilis, which was treatable. (Shakespeare was treated for it.) The unlucky musicians likely felled by the sexually transmitted infection included Schubert, Donizetti, Schumann, Smetana, Wolf, Joplin, and Delius.

## GORY DETAIL

SOMEWHERE BETWEEN 150,000 AND 220,000 PEOPLE DIED AS A RESULT OF THE ATOMIC BOMBS DROPPED ON HIROSHIMA AND NAGASAKI, JAPAN. THE HEAT OF THE BLAST WAS SO INTENSE THAT IT LEFT BEHIND "SHADOW" IMPRINTS OF PEOPLE AND OBJECTS THAT WERE VAPORIZED INSTANTLY.

## MAN VS. NATURE

Natural disasters cause tens of thousands of deaths each year, but human beings far outpace nature in deadliness. Global homicides alone account for nearly 500,000 deaths. Factoring in wars and other conflicts, there's no contest—estimates put the total global death toll of war throughout history at as much as 1 billion.

## STALIN VS. HITLER: BATTLE ROYALE

The deadliest battle in history, the Battle of Stalingrad during World War II, lasted more than five months and took the lives of 1.2 million people. It just goes to show how successful two battling genocidal maniacs can be when they put their mind to something.

## A LITTLE OVERPROTECTIVE

Kamikaze pilots—the Japanese soldiers who flew suicidal missions in World War II to take out targets using their own planes—wore helmets on the way down.

## THE DOGS OF WAR

Estimates put the body count of World War II at around 60 million: 15 million soldiers and a completely insane 45 million civilians. In comparison, the Vietnam War resulted in 3.8 million deaths, and the Korean War caused 3 million more. That's a lot of destruction caused by a handful of megalomaniacal guys.

## SPITTING IN DR. JENNER'S FACE

No record of historical deaths would be complete without the 2020 pandemic that made vaccines controversial after a successful 224-year run. The coronavirus (aka COVID-19) has killed roughly 7 million people and counting.

"I'M BORED WITH IT ALL."

WINSTON CHURCHILL'S LAST WORDS

# THE NOT-SO-CIVIL WAR

## A SOMEWHAT PREDICTABLE OUTCOME

Of the 620,000 recorded military deaths during the Civil War, about two-thirds have been attributed to disease and not something more obvious, like cannons. Crowded conditions, poor hygiene, terrible diets, and lack of proper medical care were a recipe for disaster, not just stomach problems.

## THEY DID THEM DIRTY

Two of the biggest killers of soldiers in the Civil War were diarrhea and dysentery, with a total of 57,000 kills. Why? Because the soldiers, in all their battle wisdom, constructed latrines close to the water, which contaminated it for anyone downstream.

## GORY DETAIL

THE BATTLE OF ANTIETAM, WHICH IS CONSIDERED ONE OF THE BLOODIEST DAYS IN AMERICAN HISTORY, RESULTED IN OVER 23,000 CASUALTIES. BY THE END OF IT, THE SUNKEN STREET ON WHICH IT TOOK PLACE WAS BRIMMING WITH THE BODIES OF THE DEAD AND WOUNDED TO THE POINT THAT THE SOIL BECAME SOAKED WITH BLOOD, EARNING IT A LOVELY NEW NAME: BLOODY LANE.

## SPREADING THE WEALTH

Troops on the move also brought diseases like smallpox, measles, and mumps to rural areas that hadn't experienced them before and therefore had little medical knowledge or resources to treat them.

## AN INFAMOUS MONIKER

Childhood maladies weren't the only things getting around. In 1863, Union general Joseph Hooker invited prostitutes into the soldiers' encampments to improve morale. The decision was a boon for STDs, with more than 100,000 cases of gonorrhea and close to 80,000 cases of syphilis reported among the troops. Plus, Hooker's name became forever associated with the oldest profession.

## · DUMB WAYS ⟿ DIE ·

Twenty-four-year-old American actress Martha Mansfield was filming the Civil War drama *The Warrens of Virginia* in the early 1920s when a careless crew member tossed a lit match in her direction. Her costume went up in flames, engulfing her, and she died from the burns at the hospital the next day. (That's surely just one of the many dangers of hoop skirts.)

# CHAPTER 3

# THE MAGIC OF MORTICIANS

UNDERTAKER, FUNERAL DIRECTOR, EMBALMER—A MORTICIAN BY
ANY OTHER NAME WOULD STILL SMELL LIKE DEATH AND EMPATHY.
THESE MULTITALENTED FOLKS ARE PART SMALL-BUSINESS OWNER,
PART MAKEUP ARTIST, PART SCIENTIST, PART THERAPIST,
PART PARTY PLANNER, AND ALL CHILL. FROM
COLLECTING AND PREPARING BODIES TO
BURNING THEM UP, NOTHING RUFFLES
THEIR POLYETHYLENE COVERALLS.
PREPARE TO BE AMAZED!

# A Defining Role

## IT'S ALL ABOUT BRANDING

Because the original term for someone who cared for dead bodies—"undertaker"—creeped people out, tastemakers in the funeral industry put out a call for alternatives in *Embalmer's Monthly*. The winner was the more customer-friendly *mortician*.

## MORTICIAN, IT IS

"Mortician," "funeral director," "embalmer," and "undertaker" can all refer to the same person, or each title can refer to a different person. Generally speaking, the funeral director takes the front of house (customer service) and the undertaker handles the back of house (body transport and prep). Embalmer is pretty self-explanatory.

## JACK OF ALL TRADES

A mortician's work can include filing paperwork, dealing with the family, and planning the festivities; transporting, washing, embalming, and dressing the body; casketing the body and applying the makeup; and arranging flowers, writing obituaries, and generally running the show. In other words, all the things.

## SPECIAL EDUCATION

Besides nerves of steel, funeral direction requires a college degree in mortuary science, a license, at least a year-long internship or apprenticeship, continuing education, and a serious work ethic.

..........

## SOMEONE START RECRUITING

There are only about 24,000 funeral directors in the United States. Considering the number of dead bodies that drop every year—2.7 million, if you recall—that doesn't really feel like enough. (Hint: It's not. Be nice to your overworked neighborhood morticians.)

## · DUMB WAYS ᴛᴏ DIE ·

The unending and ever-surprising stupidity of human beings keeps morticians busy in between natural deaths. For example, at least ten people have been killed by gender-reveal parties. And that number is sure to get bigger as the idiotic stunts—like DIY colored explosives—do.

## BREAKING THE GLASS EPITAPH

In a field once dominated by men, women now make up more than 70 percent of mortuary-science graduates. (If you're going to be expected to clean up everyone's mess anyway, you may as well get paid averagely for it.)

> "LIFE DOES NOT CEASE TO BE FUNNY WHEN PEOPLE DIE ANY MORE THAN IT CEASES TO BE SERIOUS WHEN PEOPLE LAUGH."
>
> GEORGE BERNARD SHAW

## A GOOD EXCUSE

It's hard to have a life when you work with the dead. People don't die on a 9-to-5 schedule, which means morticians work weekends and holidays, have to be on-call several nights a week, and constantly cancel plans. A mortician may not be your most reliable friend, but they'll definitely have the most interesting gossip.

## DEALING WITH DEADLINES

Morticians have to plan entire funeral events with 24 to 48 hours' notice while dealing with grieving families. You don't know a hard deadline until you've dealt with the dead!

## SHOW THEM THE MONEY

The average annual salary for a mortician in the United States is $59,000, which definitely isn't enough for all the hours they put in (or the twice-a-week therapy sessions the job probably necessitates).

........

## JUST A CAT NAP

Between the stress and the hours, it's not surprising that morticians have been known to occasionally nap in showroom caskets. But they must be pretty desperate for some shut-eye, because caskets aren't actually comfortable for the living. That thin mattress is usually sitting on metal springs.

## GORY DETAIL

IF THE GRIEVING FAMILIES AND GRUELING HOURS DON'T GET TO YOU, THE MANGLED BODIES AND MURDER VICTIMS MIGHT. NOT EVERYONE IS LUCKY ENOUGH TO DIE IN THEIR SLEEP AT THE RIPE OLD AGE OF NINETY-EIGHT. A MORTICIAN'S JOB IS OFTEN TO MAKE BODIES VIEWABLE NO MATTER THEIR CONDITION.

# BODIES ON THE MOVE

### HIDING IN PLAIN SIGHT

Soccer moms and funeral directors have something in common: a love of minivans. The vans are an easier, more discreet mode of transport for bodies than the hearses that lead more formal funeral processions.

### A LITTLE HELP

Although morticians do a lot of the heavy lifting themselves, they also have options for more cumbersome pickups. If they can't load a body on their own, they'll call in nurses, security guards, or whoever is around for help. They've even been known to call in firefighters and police.

### BETTER SAFE THAN SORRY

Caskets have locks not due to fear of a zombie apocalypse, but because of how far they have to travel—from the funeral home to the church to the graveyard. No one wants that casket to pop open while the pallbearers are carrying it.

# FIRST THINGS FIRST: SETTING THE FEATURES

## THAT NATURAL LOOK ISN'T NATURAL

The first step in preserving a body for viewing isn't embalming. It's creating that comforting peaceful expression on a loved one's face (called "setting the features") before the embalming process sets the tissue in place.

## KEEP THOSE CHEEKBONES HIGH

Like everything else in the body, facial features sag after death (and before death, if you're lucky enough to get old). Morticians have to give cheekbones a little help with cotton or small plastic pieces called "expression formers" to keep the cheeks where they're supposed to be.

### · DUMB WAYS TO DIE ·

The first emperor of China, Qin Shi Huang, was so afraid of dying that he forbade anyone to talk about death under the penalty of . . . death. He began drinking an elixir of mercury he thought would keep him alive forever. He died of mercury poisoning at age forty-nine.

## FILLER UP!

Plastic surgeons weren't the first to use fillers to add a youthful glow to faces. Morticians have long been injecting tissue fillers into lips, noses, cheeks, eyebrows, chins, hands, and wrinkles to get bodies back into pre-mortem condition. Or as close to it as they can get.

## DISPOSABLE LENSES INDEED

Worried about your contact lenses sticking to your eyeballs after death like they do after a nap? No need. If you die while wearing lenses, the mortician takes them out while prepping your eyes.

## LIKE PULLING TEETH

Similarly, you won't be buried with dentures in place because morticians have other plans for your mouth. (Just wait!) If your family doesn't want the dentures, they might get stuffed into the lining of your casket to spend eternity with you.

........

## START SMILING NOW (OR DON'T)

If you had resting bitch face in life, you'll probably have it in death. The face settles into its natural state after you die, and without blood or oxygen to keep things mobile, it's tricky for morticians to move the facial features.

## · DUMB WAYS ᴛᴏ DIE ·

Being well rested won't necessarily save you from an early death. Around 450 people die every year from falling out of bed. Sure, most of those are very young or very old, but head and neck injuries don't discriminate.

## LEAKS HAPPEN

### KEEP YOUR CHIN UP

Morticians stuff a body's nose, throat, and mouth with cotton before inserting a plastic mouth former (to buck up lifeless lips). Then they wire, sew, or glue the mouth shut, not only to prevent leakage but also to avoid any unsettling gaping maw moments at the viewing.

### SOME EXPERT-LEVEL SEWING

If you're picturing Billy from *Hocus Pocus*, this is not that. No mortician is stitching across the lips like they have a centuries-old vendetta against the deceased. They suture inside the mouth so that when they pull on the end of the thread, the lips zip shut—and those who view the body are none the wiser.

## GORY DETAIL

AS THE BODY BEGINS TO DECOMPOSE AND LIQUEFY, THOSE UNRULY LIQUIDS RARELY STAY PUT. AND ANY ORIFICE WILL WORK AS AN ESCAPE HATCH—NOSE, MOUTH, EYEBALLS, AND OTHER, MORE SENSITIVE, AREAS.

## GETTING CRAFTY WITH LEAK PREVENTION

Morticians have a few options for plugging the leaks, depending on their persistence—from cotton balls and glue to plugs and sutures. So, yes, you may very well leave this world with your butt sewn shut.

........

## WHO'S GONNA KNOW?

As long as there aren't any special requests in the underwear department (which does happen), some morticians will opt for using adult diapers instead of stuffing butts, for obvious reasons.

## · DUMB WAYS ᴛᴏ DIE ·

Sometimes, leaks are preferable. At least four people have died in recent years from brain-eating amoebas after using a neti pot and unsterilized tap water to cleanse their sinuses. Had they imbibed the little buggers, they would have been fine. Stomach acid kills them. But the amoeba are right at home in nasal passages and prefer to go up than out.

# A Few Final Touches

## ONE LAST RUB-DOWN

You get one final massage on this earth . . . if your body gets embalmed, that is. Massage relieves the stiffening of the joints and muscles caused by rigor so the embalming process can work.

.........

## IT PUTS THE LOTION ON THE SKIN

No massage would be complete without a luxurious skin cream. Morticians slather it on to keep your skin supple and, well, positionable so they can rebuild collapsed areas with fluid or formers as needed.

.........

"I'M ALWAYS RELIEVED WHEN SOMEONE IS DELIVERING A EULOGY AND I REALIZE I'M LISTENING TO IT."

GEORGE CARLIN

## ONE SQUEAKY-CLEAN CORPSE

Embalmers wash a dead body three times: at the beginning of the process, during the actual embalming, and once more at the end. But it's not just to make sure the deceased is fresh and funeral ready. It also helps the chemicals get into every nook and cranny.

## WORK SMARTER, NOT HARDER

Morticians occasionally resort to using Super Glue to close eyes and mouths, seal cuts, and even mend broken bones in a pinch. There are mortuary-specific equivalents, but most have been known to reach for the dollar-store variety.

........

## DUCT TAPE CAN SOLVE ANY PROBLEM

Duct tape is another dollar-store find that every person alive should have on hand, but it's also helpful for the dead. Many morticians use it to keep breasts perky after molding them (just like women use "boob tape" for particular outfits).

# GORY DETAIL

MORTICIANS OCCASIONALLY CUT THE TENDONS OR MUSCLES TO CREATE A MORE NATURAL POSE, PARTICULARLY IF THE LIMBS ARE DISTORTED BY A DISEASE SUCH AS ARTHRITIS. SO IF YOU COULDN'T DO YOGA BEFORE, YOU MIGHT BE SURPRISINGLY FLEXIBLE IN THE AFTERLIFE.

# The Science of Embalming

## IT'LL KEEP (FOR A WEEK)

You can wait up to a week to embalm a body if you're not worried about it looking fresh and rosy for a viewing—for example, if embalming is required to cross state lines (which it often is). But funeral homes try to embalm a decedent within twenty-four hours, before they begin to bloat and decompose in earnest.

## EVER THE ENTREPRENEURS

The process of embalming generally takes an hour and a half to two hours—so, as long as your average rom-com. That's why a fair number of morticians do embalming work as a side hustle.

## GORY DETAIL

THE PROCESS OF EMBALMING INVOLVES DRAINING BLOOD FROM THE BODY AND REPLACING IT WITH CHEMICALS MEANT TO PRESERVE THE BODY (AS MUCH AS NATURE ALLOWS, WHICH ISN'T MUCH) FOR VIEWING, BURIAL, AND TRANSPORT USING A SPECIAL CENTRIFUGAL MACHINE.

# GORY DETAIL

## A THOROUGH JOB

After draining the blood and embalming the arteries, morticians individually puncture and embalm every intact organ using a trocar (hollow syringe) in a process called "cavity embalming." Then they plug the holes with plastic trocar buttons.

## WHAT A WASTE

The blood—and whatever else is brewing in the body as decomp sets in—goes down the drain and into the municipal sewage system with all the other wastewater. (Well, where else is it supposed to go?)

## KEEP YOUR BACTERIA TO YOURSELF

Embalming fluid (formaldehyde) kills most bacteria, diseases, and fungi, which is why it's required for anyone who dies from a communicable disease. But more serious diseases, such as Ebola, mean skipping over embalming and sealing the diseased body in a leak-proof bag and hermetically sealed casket.

## THEY CAN'T SEE YOUR LIVER (OR LACK THEREOF)

You can still be embalmed and have a viewing if you choose to donate your organs upon your death. After all, you barely have eyeballs at that point, and nobody would know it thanks to morticians.

## NATURAL CAUSES, YOU SAY?

Embalming pretty much obliterates evidence of foul play. So if there's even a hint of suspicion around a person's cause of death, you'll want to skip embalming and give authorities a fighting chance should they need to exhume the body later.

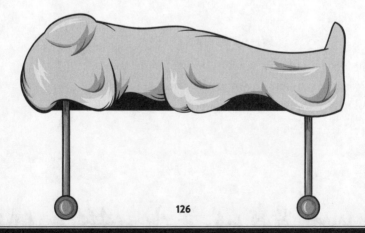

# THE ART OF EMBALMING

## LIKE PHOTOSHOP FOR BODIES

Embalming isn't always necessary. In fact, it's very rarely necessary. But it can come in handy when you need to correct typical dead-body issues such as emaciation, edema, bloating, bruising, wounds, skin discoloration, and even fading hair color.

..........

## FULL OF LIFE (OR SOMETHING)

On the plus side, if a decedent is emaciated from a long illness, the embalmer can plump them up to look more like themselves—a comfort to their grieving family.

## · DUMB WAYS TO DIE ·

Beauty is in the eye of the beholder, which in case of dead bodies, is often the embalmer. But imagine if they looked at their hard work and burst out laughing. Supposedly, that's how Greek painter Zeuxis met his end. He died of laughter when he beheld his own painting of the goddess Aphrodite. To be fair, the elderly woman who commissioned it had insisted on posing for it.

## LOOKING GREEN AROUND THE GILLS

The downside is that the formaldehyde in embalming fluid can give the body a greenish-gray tint, which is why the right clothes, makeup, and lighting are viewing essentials.

## A CREATIVE SOLUTION

That chemical tint isn't the only problem. Blood gives the skin its "in living color" look, so the absence of blood after embalming can make a person look washed out. To combat both, embalmers add a bit of custom-colored dye to the solution.

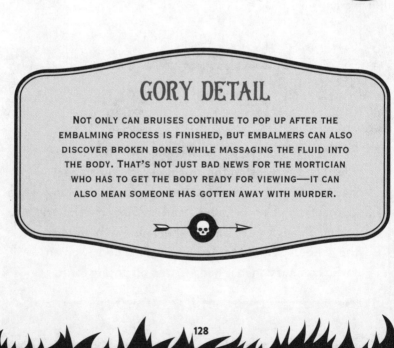

## GORY DETAIL

NOT ONLY CAN BRUISES CONTINUE TO POP UP AFTER THE EMBALMING PROCESS IS FINISHED, BUT EMBALMERS CAN ALSO DISCOVER BROKEN BONES WHILE MASSAGING THE FLUID INTO THE BODY. THAT'S NOT JUST BAD NEWS FOR THE MORTICIAN WHO HAS TO GET THE BODY READY FOR VIEWING—IT CAN ALSO MEAN SOMEONE HAS GOTTEN AWAY WITH MURDER.

# FORMALDEHYDE IS FOREVER

## QUITE THE WARNING LABEL

The EPA considers formaldehyde toxic waste. Long-term exposure to low levels in the air or on the skin can cause respiratory problems and skin irritation, not to mention cancer. And ingesting the stuff is just plain fatal.

## WELL-PRESERVED SOIL

Funeral homes go through 5.3 million gallons of embalming fluid each year, almost all of which ends up in the soil or the air at some point. (That's not at all concerning, given the previous information.)

## GREEN EMBALMING IS A THING

Thankfully, the eco-friendly funeral movement is gaining momentum and bringing with it safer alternatives. Newer embalming fluids skip the formaldehyde in favor of essential oils and may even preserve the body for longer.

"THOSE WHO WELCOME DEATH HAVE ONLY TRIED IT FROM THE EARS UP"

—WILSON MIZNER

## A LITTLE NIP/TUCK

If you've always been curious about liposuction, you may yet have your chance to experience it—albeit not consciously. Morticians will use a needle to aspirate any excess fluid and combat unsightly bloating that might upset loved ones or result in leakage (also upsetting).

## A BIT EXTREME

Yes, embalmers can pose a body so that it sits up for viewing. But "extreme embalming"—as it's logically called—takes four times as long, costs twice as much, requires stronger (read: more toxic) embalming fluid, and is only performed by a handful of providers.

# YOUR BODY, YOUR CHOICE

## YOU NEED A COOLING-OFF PERIOD

Roughly half of all people are embalmed, which means half aren't. Unembalmed bodies just need to be refrigerated until the viewing to slow down decomposition (but the sooner they can be buried, the better for everyone involved, obviously).

## SOMETIMES LESS IS MORE

Many morticians and funeral-goers think that bodies look better without embalming than with it. And—bonus—all they require for preparation is a little lotion on their now moisture-devoid faces, which saves everyone time and money.

## GORY DETAIL

A CLOSED CASKET DOESN'T GUARANTEE A LACK OF ODOR, ESPECIALLY IF THE BODY HASN'T BEEN EMBALMED. JUST IMAGINE A ROTTING PIECE OF FRUIT IN THE FRIDGE. FROM ADDING AIR FRESHENERS AND KITTY LITTER TO THE CASKET TO SITTING CITRONELLA CANDLES AROUND IT (ROTTING BODIES ATTRACT BUGS), MORTICIANS HAVE TO GET CREATIVE SO LOVED ONES DON'T NOTICE ANYTHING NOXIOUS.

# GLAM SQUAD GOALS

## NO SUCH THING AS MINT CONDITION

A mortician's makeup skills are referred to as "restorative art" because even the freshest bodies have already begun their inevitable (and fast-moving) decline. So making your deceased relative look like the person you knew and loved in life is a little like restoring an old car to its former glory—if the car was slowly imploding.

## LOOK ALIVE!

Making a body look fresh-faced and dewy requires the same variety of products that most women have on hand on a regular Tuesday: makeup brushes, concealer, foundation, color-correcting palettes, blurring and setting powders, blush, lipstick, and mascara. But because mortuary makeup is an art, morticians also use paint brushes to get that "just sleeping" look.

## FREE MAKEOVER, ANYONE?

Thanks to that hands-on experience, morticians are often the go-to person for all their friends' and families' hair and makeup needs, from product recommendations to dye jobs. If they can make the dead look good, imagine what they can do with someone who has a pulse.

## TALK ABOUT SMUDGE-PROOF

Unlike the makeup you find at drugstores, which are thermogenic and require heat to blend, mortuary cosmetics are non-thermogenic, which means they easily blend on cold skin. You know who else uses non-thermogenic makeup? Stage actors who don't want their meticulously applied faces melting under the hot spotlights.

..........

## JUST IMAGINE THE REWARD POINTS

That said, morticians are just as likely to hit up Sephora as they are to order makeup from mortuary-specific vendors to make sure they have the best products for the job. Although morticians can blend makeup to get the right skin tone, retailers tend to offer a wider variety of ready-to-use shades.

## · DUMB WAYS TO DIE ·

A fair number of bodies can't be restored for viewing and are tucked neatly into closed caskets instead. For example, John Bowen, who was struck by a flying lawn mower during an ill-fated aerial show at a 1979 Jets game, was probably a lost cause. (New fear of drones unlocked.)

## ONE MORE LICENSE CAN'T HURT

Not every mortician is Bobbi Brown, although some do top off their extensive coursework with a cosmetology license. Thankfully, families can bring in their own hairstylists, makeup artists, and nail technicians if they choose to (and if the professionals are willing, which is a pretty big "if").

## EVERYONE LOVES A CANDID SHOT

Morticians use pictures provided by family members to guide their work on the decedent's appearance, so annual headshots might not be a terrible idea. Aunt Bea's face from the 2000s is probably going to look weird done up in Aunt Bea's look from the 1950s.

## THE HAIR ON YOUR CHINNY CHIN CHIN

Because some people are very attached to their loved one's appearance, a mortician will even ask if you want Grandma's chin hairs removed. (But do consider what Grandma would want, which is probably *not* for every mourner to see her un-tweezed chin.)

"THE IDEA
IS TO
DIE YOUNG
AS LATE
AS POSSIBLE."

—ASHLEY MONTAGU

## GORY DETAIL

THE THIN SKIN ON HANDS CAN MAKE RESTORATION AND POSITIONING TRICKY BECAUSE THE TOP LAYERS SEPARATE FROM THE LOWER LAYERS, SLIP, AND EVEN SLOUGH OFF IN WHAT'S CALLED "GLOVE FORMATION"—AS IN, YOU COULD WEAR THE SKIN LIKE A GLOVE. EMBALMING FLUID CAN HELP KEEP IT IN PLACE, EVEN IF JUST APPLIED TOPICALLY. MORTICIANS ALSO USE WOUND FILLER AND MAKEUP TO COVER UP ANY TEARS.

## NO GOODBYE KISS

A good mortician will disinfect brushes with every use, but there's no guarantee that the one used on Uncle Ed's face wasn't used on hundreds of other dead guys. So keep your lips to yourself at the funeral.

## CHECK MY NAILS

Because the decedent's hands are usually visible during a viewing, folded neatly over the abdomen, they get the same special treatment as the face. That means restoration, makeup, and even a full manicure.

# A Guaranteed Good Hair Day

### TALK ABOUT HAIR STANDING ON END

Hair is a protein, which means it stiffens up with embalming too. The best morticians know to comb the hair forward before it sets so it doesn't fall flat during the viewing. (Kind of like what women did to their bangs in the '80s, but better.)

### ONE FINAL BLOWOUT

If it's been a minute since you've been to the salon when you die, you're in good hands with a mortician. They'll clean up your cut, color your roots, and even give you some dimensional highlights—using a can of spray paint made for the purpose.

### THE ULTIMATE NON-PERMANENT DYE

Mortuary hair dye is water based, which makes it easy to do color corrections on the spot. All the mortician has to do is wash out the dye and start fresh.

# WHEN FOUNDATION JUST ISN'T ENOUGH

### FIXING YOUR FACE

Mortuary makeup isn't just cosmetic—it has to compensate for the lack of blood flow to the face and give it that rosy, "I have a pulse" color. Whether or not you're the kind of person to put on a full face of makeup, you will be when you die.

### NOT EVERYONE CAN ROCK A RED LIP

The goal of makeup is to look as natural as possible, but that's a lot easier when the decedent wore makeup to begin with. People who went *au naturale* in life—especially men—look strange with lipstick on if it's not properly applied. But it *will* be applied.

## GORY DETAIL

ANYONE WITH LIGHT TRAUMA TO THE FACE (OR OTHER VISIBLE AREA) GETS A SPECIAL TREAT: A NEW ONE MADE AT LEAST PARTIALLY OUT OF MORTUARY WAX. MORTICIANS WORK THE PUTTY-LIKE SUBSTANCE INTO GASHES AND HOLES AND EVEN USE IT TO RE-CREATE MISSING SKIN AND CARTILAGE (LIKE NOSES).

## AIRBRUSHING: NOT JUST FOR INFOMERCIALS

Heavy bruising requires special techniques and tools, like an airbrush. (Just ask anyone with dark under-eye circles.) The mortician will spray the decedent's skin with a base color before applying color to help the injured area blend in seamlessly.

## DON'T LOSE YOUR HEAD

Head reconstruction is a standard part of the mortuary-science curriculum. Students will practice on dummy heads during intensive multiple-day labs, creating facial features, smashing and reassembling plaster skulls, and restoring a disturbingly lifelike head with trauma. (Honestly, it sounds more fun than statistics classes.)

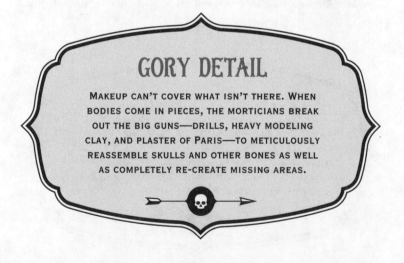

## GORY DETAIL

MAKEUP CAN'T COVER WHAT ISN'T THERE. WHEN BODIES COME IN PIECES, THE MORTICIANS BREAK OUT THE BIG GUNS—DRILLS, HEAVY MODELING CLAY, AND PLASTER OF PARIS—TO METICULOUSLY REASSEMBLE SKULLS AND OTHER BONES AS WELL AS COMPLETELY RE-CREATE MISSING AREAS.

# SMOKE AND MIRRORS AND CASKETS

### DOWN TO THE LAST DETAIL

Morticians carefully consider every little detail, down to the position of the zipper on the casket pillow (facing the back of the casket) and the creases on the deceased's clothing.

### LIKE ROSE-COLORED GLASSES

Even when the mortician has done everything they can to make the deceased look good, it's still a dead body. So funeral homes light caskets using pink bulbs to help diffuse the light and gloss over any imperfections.

### BASKING IN THE GLOW (MOSTLY)

One of several reasons for the split casket lid (called a "half-couch" casket) is that it's easier to give the deceased's face a rosy glow than it is to light the whole body in a way that's more comforting than off-putting.

## UP IN ARMS

Getting the arms and hands into position can take a little doing. Morticians place foam support blocks under the arms and will use anything from Super Glue to hair ties to keep the hands crossed over the corpse's abdomen.

........

## BEING CHEAP COMES AT A COST

Less expensive caskets create more work for funeral directors, who have to do things like pad the foot area so the body doesn't slide down the cheap plastic lining mid-funeral. If you're not sure about your mortician's commitment to the craft, consider opting for a higher-quality casket.

### · DUMB WAYS TO DIE ·

A lot of things are not what they seem, like a supposedly unbreakable window. In 1993, Garry Hoy found that out the hard way by throwing himself at one such window—fully expecting to bounce off it like he had done dozens of times before—only for the glass to pop out of the frame. Garry plummeted to his death from the twenty-fourth floor.

## IT'S TOUGH BEING TALL

If the deceased is too tall for the casket, the mortician will place something under their knees to create an imperceptible bend. But given that the standard casket has an interior length of 78 to 79 inches, they'd probably have to be a Harlem Globetrotter to need it.

........

## GO TO THE MATTRESSES

Casket mattresses may boast the same polyfill or memory foam as your favorite topper, but it's meant to keep a body in place, not to keep one comfy. The mattress is mainly used to conceal thin metal strips or particle board.

........

## IT'S A RENTAL

Rental caskets (used for a viewing before the body is cremated) look just like regular caskets but come with removable inserts and single-use liners so that anything one body touches gets tossed before the casket is used again. The casket itself is also rigorously cleaned.

"DEATH IS NATURE'S WAY OF SAYING, 'YOUR TABLE IS READY.'"

—ROBIN WILLIAMS

# All Dressed Up with Nowhere to Go

### STAYING IN MEANS NO MAKEUP

A body is prepped and dressed the same way whether the casket is open or closed, but the mortician probably won't bother doing their hair and makeup if no one is going to see it.

### A SURREPTITIOUS SNIP

Morticians usually cut the decedent's clothing down the back to make it easier to dress the body without jostling it (read: possibly causing leakage). So if you ask for Great Grandma's dress back after the viewing (and people do), just know that you'll be getting it in pieces.

### MODEST CLOTHING MAKES LIGHT(ER) WORK

If you ever supply the clothing for a corpse, do the mortician a favor and provide an outfit with a high neckline and long sleeves. They prefer as much coverage as possible because anything that's not covered has to be cosmeticized.

## BRAS ARE OPTIONAL

Although socks and underwear are not required, most morticians will ask a family member to provide them for the deceased. It's just polite. But if you don't want to be buried with a bra, the mortician will respect your wishes. (And if you're embalmed, you won't need a bra to keep things in place anyway.)

## PUTTING YOUR BEST ... FOOT ... FORWARD

If you do opt for a bra but not embalming, the mortician will probably pad the bra to help keep your breasts looking perky for the viewing. (And you thought you were done with padding when you graduated junior high.)

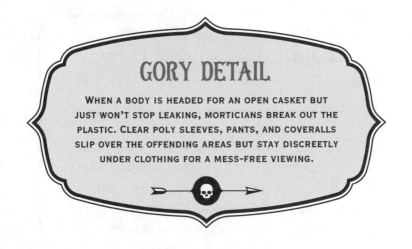

## GORY DETAIL

WHEN A BODY IS HEADED FOR AN OPEN CASKET BUT JUST WON'T STOP LEAKING, MORTICIANS BREAK OUT THE PLASTIC. CLEAR POLY SLEEVES, PANTS, AND COVERALLS SLIP OVER THE OFFENDING AREAS BUT STAY DISCREETLY UNDER CLOTHING FOR A MESS-FREE VIEWING.

## ANGELS WITH SEWING MACHINES

There is a program called Angel Gown® that provides support to families who have lost a baby—in particular, burial gowns made by volunteer seamstresses around the world from the fabric of donated wedding gowns.

## THAT'S JUST SWELL

When you choose an outfit for your deceased loved one, don't bother with the shoes. (Unless you want them to be buried wearing Crocs, probably.) Your feet swell when you die, making it difficult for shoes to fit. That's one more reason to opt for a half-couch casket.

## · DUMB WAYS ⥱ DIE ·

Just like superhero capes are a hazard, so are scarves. At least, they can be when you're driving a convertible. That's how famous dancer Isadora Duncan met her maker. Her long silk scarf was blowing in the wind when it got caught in the car's hubcap, strangled her, and whipped her out of the car and onto the road.

## WHO DOESN'T LOVE POCKETS?

Many caskets have secret compartments in which to hide personal mementos. Some also come with a "memory tube"—a plastic vial that contains identifying information but fits into the outside of the coffin and looks like a decorative screw. If the casket should migrate, the vial eliminates the need to open it up to find out who's inside.

## ONE FOR THE ROAD

Friends and family can ask that pretty much anything be buried with their loved one, from their trademark glasses to their childhood clarinet and even a beloved pet's cremains. The decedent can also stipulate in their will what they plan to try to take with them.

## GORY DETAIL

YOU CAN ALSO ASK FOR THINGS BACK BEFORE THE COFFIN IS SEALED, LIKE THE JEWELRY YOUR LOVED ONE WORE FOR THE FUNERAL. IT'S NOT A PRETTY THOUGHT, BUT A ROTTING BODY OR BONY SKELETON DOESN'T NEED BLING. YOU, HOWEVER, CAN ENJOY THOSE HEIRLOOMS WHILE YOU'RE STILL NORTH OF THE GRASS.

# A Mortician's Work Is Never Done

## LIFE IS BRIEF, TO-DO LISTS ARE NOT

A mortician who runs their own funeral home might also be in charge of setting up for viewings and services, which means arranging announcements, transportation, seating, decorations, and counseling. In case spending several hours on the body wasn't enough work.

## EXPECT THE UNEXPECTED

They'll also need to be around to solve any problems that pop up, from running out of tissues to dealing with family squabbles. In 1845, President Andrew Jackson's pet parrot had to be removed from his funeral for swearing.

## THAT'S A SERIOUSLY LONG DAY

Once the viewing is over and everyone has seen the mortician's handiwork, they still have to wrap things up. That means putting away the chairs, donating the flowers, and preparing the body for cremation or travel if it's not ending the day six feet under.

"DON'T SEND ME FLOWERS WHEN I'M DEAD. IF YOU LIKE ME, SEND THEM WHILE I'M ALIVE."

—BRIAN CLOUGH

## AND IT KEEPS GETTING LONGER

To prepare a body for cremation, the mortician has to undress the dead, clean them again, wrap them in a white sheet, and transfer them to a combustible container (like a cardboard cremation casket). Sometimes, they even do the cremating themselves.

·········

## ARTS AND CRAFTS, ANYONE?

Then, not only do morticians have to transfer the cremains to any purchased urns, they might even have to put them together. Some biodegradable urns come with things like bags, boxes, twine, and decorations that need to be assembled. (But the end result is very pretty!)

### · DUMB WAYS ᴛᴏ DIE ·

Some people—like morticians—are just overachievers. Take Sergey Tuganov, for example. In 2009, he bet two women he could last for twelve hours in bed with them, guzzled a bottle of Viagra, and died of a heart attack. He did win the bet first, though. So that's something.

148

# CHAPTER 4

# THE MARCH TO THE GRAVE

DEATH IS INEVITABLE, BUT HOW YOU'LL GET THERE IS ANYONE'S GUESS. FROM ILLNESS AND INJURY TO HUBRIS AND STUPIDITY, THERE ARE A PLETHORA OF WAYS TO GO. LUCKILY, WE HAVE THOUSANDS OF YEARS OF SCIENCE, STATISTICS, AND STORIES TO HELP US FIGURE OUT WHICH ACTIVITIES ARE MOST LIKELY TO SHOVE US OFF THIS MORTAL COIL, AND THIS CHAPTER LETS YOU IN ON THEM.

# WHISTLING PAST THE GRAVEYARD

### ADULT SUPERVISION REQUIRED

Kids begin to understand the concept of death as young as two years old but don't understand its permanence until age nine, which is part of why they will try to float down from roofs via umbrella like Mary Poppins with zero concern for their own safety.

### DAREDEVILS ARE BORN, NOT MADE

That interest in the death defying doesn't always go away with a fully formed prefrontal cortex. Humans have been hardwired to push their limits since the early days of mankind, when competition for things like food and shelter was literally fierce.

## · DUMB WAYS TO DIE ·

Reynisfjara beach in Iceland is the perfect example of the ways in which we humans flirt with death. Despite warnings with blinking lights posted everywhere due to a mixture of strong waves, dangerous undercurrents, and jagged rocks, people still play in the waves like they're at the Jersey Shore. The spot averages nearly one death a year.

# EVEN BORING STUFF CAN KILL YOU

## NOISE IS KILLING US

Sounds from planes and trains create a risk of hypertension, stroke, and heart attacks—and you don't get used to the constant loud noise. Studies have shown that prolonged exposure just triggers the body more, worsening the negative effects. On the plus side, you have an excuse to skip that heavy metal concert.

## A SPLITTING HEADACHE

Loud noises don't always take the slow route to kill you; they can sometimes kill you immediately. Sure, it's rare, but human heads can start bursting at sounds above 240 decibels. Anything over 150 decibels is usually produced by massive explosions or rocket launches.

## SLEEP IS NON-NEGOTIABLE

Chronic sleep deprivation (aka the average American's sleep schedule) can lead to all sorts of fun things, like obesity, heart problems, and a perma-nently bad mood. But going without sleep for as few as three days can lead to psychosis and death.

"I'M NOT AFRAID OF DEATH; I JUST DON'T WANT TO BE THERE WHEN IT HAPPENS."

—WOODY ALLEN

## LOOK BOTH WAYS

A pedestrian is killed by a motor vehicle every eighty-eight minutes in the United States. That's about sixteen people a day or, to put it in perspective, a large dinner party's worth of guests not making it to dessert ("dessert" being old age, in this scenario).

## THAT ESCALATED QUICKLY

An average of 30 people die each year from elevator and escalator injuries, and another 17,000 are seriously injured. Loose shoelaces, distracted steps, and sudden stops contribute to an alarming number of accidents—some fatally embarrassing, others just fatal.

### · DUMB WAYS TO DIE ·

Even drinking too much water can take you out. One twenty-nine-year-old woman died of water toxicity in 2007 after drinking two gallons of water in three hours during a radio contest for a gaming console. (Basically, it flushes all of the sodium out of your system and makes your cells swell up.)

## CHEW CAREFULLY

You might not think of your dinner as a deadly weapon, but statistics show that the odds of fatally choking on your food are 1 in 2,659, which makes it disturbingly common. Suddenly mindful eating seems urgent rather than indulgent.

## TIME CAN'T HEAL EVERY BROKEN HEART

"Broken heart syndrome" isn't just the basis for most country songs. It's a real thing—specifically, stress-induced cardiomyopathy. The heart muscle becomes weak under severe emotional stress. Most people recover, but some suffer severe heart muscle failure (aka death).

## FIGHT, FLIGHT, OR HEART FAILURE

You really can be scared to death! Even without an underlying heart condition, stress hormones released during a moment of intense fear can stun the heart into failure. Luckily, it's rare and, more often than not, treatable. But maybe skip the haunted house just to be on the safe side.

## NOTHING TO SNEEZE AT

Contrary to what you heard from that kid in your fifth-grade class, you *can* sneeze with your eyes open without deadly repercussions. But violent sneezes have been responsible for several deaths, particularly when they've happened to people while driving.

## THE LAST LAUGH

Laughter isn't always the best medicine. Vigorous giggles have been known to trigger cardiac arrest and asphyxiation. One British man had a fatal fit of laughter while watching a sitcom in 1975. His wife later wrote to the stars of the show to thank them for making his last thirty minutes on Earth enjoyable.

"DYING IS EASY. COMEDY IS HARD."
—EDMUND GWENN

# EVERYONE HAS A VICE

## EAT YOUR VEGETABLES

An apple a day keeps the Grim Reaper away, but that guy loves his junk food. Obesity-related conditions like heart disease, stroke, type 2 diabetes, and cancer are some of the leading causes of preventable death.

.........

## IT REALLY SHAKES YOUR FAITH

An expanding waistline isn't the only way fast food can get you. In 2022, three people died in Tacoma, Washington, after drinking listeria-riddled milkshakes from a local fast-food joint. The cause: a milkshake machine that wasn't cleaned properly (or probably at all).

## · DUMB WAYS ᴛᴏ DIE ·

An average of twelve people die every year from being crushed by a vending machine. Considering that the things weigh nearly 1,000 pounds, that's not totally preposterous. So think twice about jostling that stuck snack loose or reaching in for a freebie.

## STEP AWAY FROM THE LIGHTER

Despite warnings on packs of cigarettes—like the oh-so-subtle "Smoking will kill you"—this smelly habit still accounts for one in five deaths annually in the United States. One in five! Plus, it makes your lungs look like shriveled coal briquettes.

## DESIGNATED DRIVERS FOR THE WIN

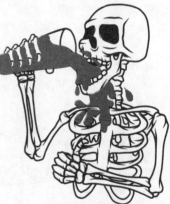

Americans love a cocktail, but alcohol is a contributing factor in around 95,000 deaths annually, which makes it the third-highest cause of preventable deaths in the United States. It's all fun and games until your liver goes on strike or you wrap your car around a tree.

## THEY CALL IT AN EPIDEMIC FOR A REASON

Doing drugs is like playing hide-and-seek with your serotonin: fun at first, but it can end with you stuck in a dark box for far too long. Over 100,000 people die from drug overdoses each year, the vast majority of which involve prescription opioids, not hard drugs like cocaine or heroin.

# YOUR BODY IS A WAR ZONE

## TAKE THIS TO HEART

Heart disease is the number-one killer in the United States, which is pretty self-explanatory when you look at our love of ultra-processed foods, obsessive working habits, and glorification of perpetual stress and busyness.

........

## PERIODS ARE THE WORST

Women are more likely to die of a heart attack than men. First, the symptoms we've been taught to watch for (chest and arm pain) are more common in men. Women tend to experience nausea, dizziness, and jaw pain. Second, women have a higher pain tolerance (and therefore ignore serious symptoms) due to years of menstrual cramps, which have been proven to be more painful than a heart attack.

........

## MAKE SOME NOISE, LADIES

Women who go to the ER with pain are more likely to be diagnosed with anxiety rather than being tested or treated for said pain, while men with similar symptoms will be given tests and medication. Not-so-astonishingly, that can lead to preventable deaths in women—especially when it comes to heart attacks.

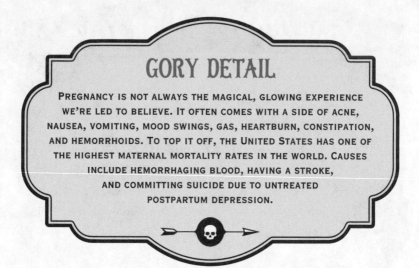

## GORY DETAIL

PREGNANCY IS NOT ALWAYS THE MAGICAL, GLOWING EXPERIENCE
WE'RE LED TO BELIEVE. IT OFTEN COMES WITH A SIDE OF ACNE,
NAUSEA, VOMITING, MOOD SWINGS, GAS, HEARTBURN, CONSTIPATION,
AND HEMORRHOIDS. TO TOP IT OFF, THE UNITED STATES HAS ONE OF
THE HIGHEST MATERNAL MORTALITY RATES IN THE WORLD. CAUSES
INCLUDE HEMORRHAGING BLOOD, HAVING A STROKE,
AND COMMITTING SUICIDE DUE TO UNTREATED
POSTPARTUM DEPRESSION.

## BIAS CAN BE DEADLY

Black women have a much higher maternal mortality rate than white
women due to deeply ingrained bias in the healthcare system. Signs
of distress are often dismissed as anxiety and exaggeration, leading to
emergencies that could have been prevented.

## TIME FOR THAT COLONOSCOPY

Cancer comes in at number two for most lethal in the United States.
Nearly 1,700 people die every day from one type or another. The good
news is that cancer deaths are down more than 30 percent over the last
30 years thanks to advancements in medicine and common sense (i.e., go
get that screening).

## IGNORANCE IS ALSO AN EPIDEMIC

HIV used to be one of the most feared and misunderstood diseases around, mostly because it was a death sentence. (Also, homophobia.) But newer drugs allow patients to live relatively normal, healthy lives and the public to focus their panic elsewhere.

.........

## DEAD BUT STILL CONTAGIOUS

Some diseases can kill not only you but also anyone who handles your body. Those include tuberculosis, bloodborne viruses (like hepatitis B and C and HIV), and gastrointestinal infections (like cholera, *E. coli*, hepatitis A, rotavirus diarrhea, salmonellosis, shigellosis, and typhoid).

### · DUMB WAYS TO DIE ·

About 7,000 people die each year due to doctors' terrible handwriting, which means that switching to digital prescriptions could save lives. (Although that gives autocorrect even more power to ruin your day.)

# THROWING IN THE CORPOREAL TOWEL

### DEATH WITH DIGNITY

Physician-assisted dying isn't like euthanizing a pet (although the same principle of ending suffering applies). Instead, the doctor prescribes a lethal dose of pills that will help the patient go peacefully. It's legal in ten states and the District of Columbia, so far, and requires patients to have a terminal illness and a prognosis of six months or fewer to live.

----------

### LOVE ACTUALLY IS ALL AROUND

Contrary to popular belief, suicide rates are actually lowest during the holidays. Turns out, being around family *isn't* the worst thing. But natural deaths increase because uncoordinated (or inebriated) people keep climbing on roofs and hanging lights.

## HELP IS AVAILABLE

No kidding—if you're struggling with your mental health, help is just a call or text away. **DIAL 988** to reach the Suicide and Crisis Lifeline, which provides free and confidential support for people in distress as well as prevention and crisis resources. You can also chat with someone on their website: **HTTPS://988LIFELINE.ORG/**.

# DON'T MESS WITH MOTHER NATURE

### WINDS OF CHANGE

Scientists estimate that climate change (think heat, storms, flooding, wildfires, and tornadoes that wouldn't be so severe had we taken those Captain Planet ads more seriously in the 1980s) has caused nearly 2 million deaths over the last 50 years.

### TURNING UP THE HEAT

Around 700 people die from heat-related causes in the United States each year, which is nothing compared to Europe's record of 70,000 heat-related deaths in a single summer in 2003. And that number is only going to climb as Mother Nature cranks up the oven.

### TOO HOT TO HANDLE

Heatstroke isn't the only concern when it comes to the mercury rising. Suicide rates have been shown to rise with every 1.8°F increase in average temperature. Some people literally can't take the heat.

## HURRICANES, TORNADOES, AND FLOODS—OH MY!

Between 1999 and 2006, heat caused more deaths than hurricanes, tornadoes, or floods in the United States. But the tables have turned, with extreme weather events now outpacing heat in the body-count department.

## FROM ONE EXTREME TO ANOTHER

Extreme temperatures contribute to roughly 5.1 million deaths globally per year. And, incredibly, the heat is the least of our worries. Of those deaths, 4.6 million are associated with *colder* temperatures, and 0.5 million are associated with hotter temperatures.

### · DUMB WAYS TO DIE ·

There's nothing wrong with a healthy appreciation for nature, but trying to keep wild animals as pets can end very badly. (Just ask Roy Horn.) Nonprofit advocacy group Born Free USA has documented more than 1,500 attacks and 75 human deaths since 1990.

## BODIES ON THE RISE

They say Lake Superior never gives up her dead. An estimated 10,000 people have died—many from 350 recorded shipwrecks—in its icy waters, which keep human remains from bloating and floating. But with climate change warming things up, those bodies may begin to decompose and rise to the surface.

## ALWAYS WEAR YOUR SPF

We may have started healing the ozone layer when we gave up the aerosol hair-spray of the 1980s, but carbon emissions (from things like gas-guzzling vehicles) aren't helping. And with increased sun exposure comes skin cancer, which is responsible for nearly 8,000 U.S. deaths per year.

"IN THIS WORLD, NOTHING CAN BE CERTAIN, EXCEPT DEATH AND TAXES."
—BENJAMIN FRANKLIN

163

# TRAVELING FROM HERE TO ETERNITY

## CRUISING INTO "RETIREMENT"

Every fun-filled cruise ship comes with its very own morgue for holding those who die at sea—an average of more than 150 people per year worldwide. Thankfully, most of those are natural deaths (which makes perfect sense when you consider the general age of cruisers).

........

## WALKING SAVES LIVES

Motor-vehicle accidents are the leading cause of death for American civilians working, living, and traveling outside of the United States. Those free walking tours are starting to sound a lot more appealing, aren't they?

## · DUMB WAYS to DIE ·

There are a lot of different ways to die when you're traveling, from looking the wrong way before crossing the street to eating something you shouldn't. But one of the dumbest has to be dying while taking a selfie. More than 300 people—and counting—have perished this way.

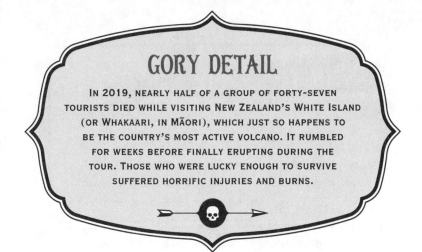

## GORY DETAIL

IN 2019, NEARLY HALF OF A GROUP OF FORTY-SEVEN TOURISTS DIED WHILE VISITING NEW ZEALAND'S WHITE ISLAND (OR WHAKAARI, IN MĀORI), WHICH JUST SO HAPPENS TO BE THE COUNTRY'S MOST ACTIVE VOLCANO. IT RUMBLED FOR WEEKS BEFORE FINALLY ERUPTING DURING THE TOUR. THOSE WHO WERE LUCKY ENOUGH TO SURVIVE SUFFERED HORRIFIC INJURIES AND BURNS.

## WATCH OUT FOR DROP BEARS

When you think about the scariest destinations on Earth, two places come to mind: Florida and Australia. Vastly different yet shockingly alike, both are full of creatures that won't blink before killing you, like alligators, crocodiles, poisonous jellyfish, venomous snakes, and kangaroos. (Yes, *kangaroos.*)

## NO SECOND CHANCES IN NATURE

There's a reason every hair dryer and tourist attraction come with explicit warnings: people are stupid. National parks like Yellowstone, Yosemite, and the Grand Canyon try to warn tourists away from interacting with murderous wildlife, sheer drops, and boiling hot springs, but they've seen 52, 126, and 134 deaths, respectively.

## · DUMB WAYS TO DIE ·

Dave Freeman, the guy who wrote *100 Things to Do Before You Die*, which recommended things like running with the bulls and bungee jumping, died an ironically uneventful death: he tripped on his hall carpet in his own house and hit his head on the wall.

## CROSS THIS OFF YOUR BUCKET LIST

Running with the bulls is a Spanish tradition that spans the country, though Pamplona attracts the most tourists. And that's just what you want when it comes to a deadly century-old pastime—*more* people. Hundreds of attendees—runners and bystanders alike—have been trampled, gored, and crushed, and dozens have died.

## NOT THE GOOD KIND OF CRUSH

At gates where the bulls are corralled into a smaller area, people can literally pile up. It's not always the crowd crush that kills you, though. Being buried under a bunch of other humans often leads to asphyxiation.

# PLANES, TRAINS, AND AUTOMOBILES

### SHOW SOME LOVE FOR AIRBAGS

Passenger cars are the second-least safe of all the standard travel options. You're seventeen times more likely to die traveling the same distance in a car as you are on a train. On the plus side, car accidents are far more survivable than train accidents.

.........

### THEY'RE CALLED "DONOR-CYCLES" FOR A REASON

Motorcycles are the most unsafe of all transportation options by far. You're roughly thirty times more likely to die on a motorcycle than in a car. (It probably has something to do with the complete lack of protective structural elements.)

## · DUMB WAYS TO DIE ·

The robots haven't taken over yet, but that doesn't mean you can trust them. Philip Paxson trusted his GPS in 2023, and it led him over a collapsed bridge and into a creek, where he tragically drowned. To his credit, there were no warning signs or barriers despite the bridge having collapsed a full nine years earlier.

## LAST STOP FOR LIFE

Train derailments get all the press, but they're extremely few and far between. Not so uncommon is a train hitting someone on the tracks. Nearly 1,000 people die each year in this type of train-related accident, and hundreds of those are suicides.

> "WHEN I DIE, I WANT TO DIE LIKE MY GRANDFATHER WHO DIED PEACEFULLY IN HIS SLEEP. NOT SCREAMING LIKE ALL THE PASSENGERS IN HIS CAR."
>
> —WILL ROGERS

## BUY THE TICKET

Despite the sheer terror of turbulence, air travel remains the safest transportation method. But your odds of dying increase as the size of your plane decreases—private and recreational planes are more likely to go down than commercial flights.

## JUST WEAR THE GOOFY VEST

Of the roughly 600 boating fatalities that happen each year, around 85 percent of victims were not wearing a life jacket. Possibly related: a large percentage of boating fatalities (roughly a third) are alcohol related.

# YOU MAY WANT TO RETHINK YOUR HOBBIES

### TRY A WALKING TOUR INSTEAD

Parasailing on the open water is a peaceful way to spend an afternoon. It's also surprisingly risky, with a disturbing number of people careening wildly into hard objects, like bridges and buildings. Over the past 30 years, the Parasail Safety Council (yes, that's a thing) has recorded 70 deaths and 1,800 injuries from parasailing gone wrong.

### A LEAP OF FAITH

Considering that more than 3 million people have jumped out of planes for fun and not because said plane was going down behind enemy lines (one of the only rational reasons for parachuting from 13,000 feet), your odds of dying while skydiving are mercifully low—1 in 300,000.

## · DUMB WAYS TO DIE ·

An afternoon of golf can be a great way to relax, right up until you accidentally catch a club or a ball to the head. But there are worse things, like bashing your club against a bench in anger over a bad shot, breaking it, and having one of the splinters pierce your heart. (RIP young Jeremy T. Brenno.)

## GORY DETAIL

THERE'S AN AVERAGE OF NINETY SCUBA-DIVING DEATHS PER YEAR IN NORTH AMERICA. RUNNING OUT OF OXYGEN IS THE MOST COMMON CAUSE, BUT THERE ARE WORSE WAYS TO GO THAN DROWNING—NAMELY, DECOMPRESSION ILLNESS, WHICH INCLUDES AN ARTERIAL GAS EMBOLISM (AGE) AND THE BENDS. BOTH INVOLVE BUBBLES BEING IN PLACES WHERE THEY DON'T BELONG, CAUSING SOMETIMES LETHAL BRAIN AND SPINAL-CORD DAMAGE.

## DANCE 'TIL YOU DROP

You're actually more likely to die at a dance party than while skydiving. (One can only assume drugs, alcohol, and heart problems have a lot to do with it.)

## DYING TO PLAY

Even less-active hobbies, like gaming, can prove dangerous. Some people get so immersed in game play that they forget to eat, drink, or sleep. As many as twenty-four have died. And then there are the two famous cases of teenage boys dropping dead in the '80s after achieving high scores in *Berserk*.

## FROZEN OR LIQUID, WATER IS DANGEROUS

The 2021–2022 ski and snowboard season made history with a ten-year high of fifty-seven fatalities—and most of those were on intermediate blue runs. But if it's any consolation, you're still 100 times more likely to die while canoeing than on the slopes.

..........

## GRAVITY ALWAYS WINS

Bungee jumping is downright docile compared with BASE jumping, which boasts 1 fatality for every 2,300 jumpers. Wingsuiting has even worse odds, which is why parachuting purists are calling for a split in the statistics. They don't want the body count on their record.

## · DUMB WAYS TO DIE ·

If anything should come with a "don't try this at home" warning, it's bungee jumping. Twenty-two-year-old Eric A. Barcia learned that the hard way when, in 1997, he taped a bunch of short bungee cords together, then tied one end around his leg and the other around the top of a railroad bridge. They found his body the next morning. He'd made the cord too long for the seventy-foot drop.

# AIN'T NO MOUNTAIN HIGH ENOUGH, APPARENTLY

## MOUNTAIN DO OR DIE

One of the deadliest things you can do is climb a mountain—even if you're experienced, healthy, agile, and fearless. In fact, that last one may be the problem. Around 1,000 daring people die climbing mountains each year.

## GET YOUR ROCKS OFF

Rock climbing is far less deadly, with only thirty deaths per year worldwide. And only 3.3 percent of climbers in the United States die, so the odds are in your favor. (If you're climbing vertical rocks, you're probably a fan of playing the odds.)

## GORY DETAIL

IT'S ESTIMATED THAT THERE ARE **200** BODIES ON MOUNT EVEREST, WHICH IS A GOOD CHUNK OF THE **322** PEOPLE WHO HAVE DIED ON THE PEAK. INCREDIBLY, HIKERS OFTEN USE THE EXPOSED BODIES AS TRAIL MARKERS.

## HAVING A MELTDOWN

The number of bodies on Mount Everest is "estimated" because many of them are buried under snow, never to be seen. But more bodies are discovered on mountains every year as the Earth warms and the snow melts.

........

## AT YOUR OWN RISK

The most common causes of death while mountain climbing are acute mountain sickness, avalanches, exhaustion, crevasses, exposure, hypothermia, and, of course, falling. In other words, a lot can go wrong when you're climbing an unforgiving, snow-covered rock.

........

## A STROKE WAITING TO HAPPEN

Mount Everest, which is the tallest peak in the world, rings in at 29,032 feet. At 26,000 feet—a height that experts lovingly call the "death zone"—the body literally begins to die cell by cell from lack of oxygen.

"I INTEND TO
LIVE FOREVER.
SO FAR,
SO GOOD."

—STEVEN WRIGHT

## GORY DETAIL

BECAUSE OF THE HIGH ALTITUDE AND LOW
TEMPERATURES, BODIES DON'T DECAY ON EVEREST.
THEY TURN BLACK AND HARD AS ROCK AND HAVE THE
POTENTIAL TO BREAK INTO PIECES IF JOSTLED, ADDING
ANOTHER FUN ELEMENT TO RETRIEVAL EFFORTS.

## TALK ABOUT A KILLER JOB

A third of the people who have died on Mount Everest were sherpas—the experienced local climbers tasked with ferrying souls safely up and down the mountain. And you thought your job sucked!

## NOBODY LEFT BEHIND (FOR A PRICE)

It's not just treacherous conditions that cause bodies to be left in place on Mount Everest. It can cost up to $100,000 to retrieve one, between the climbers and the rescue-specific gear. (If you think lifting a dead body is hard, try it when it's frozen solid.)

## MOUNTING RISK

Climate change isn't just unearthing bodies—it's also creating them. Mountain climbing is getting deadlier each year as storms and temperatures reach new extremes.

## THAT LAST STEP'S A DOOZY

If you were to commit suicide by jumping from the top of Mount Everest, or just make an unfortunate misstep, it would take a full two-and-a-half minutes for you to reach the bottom. That's a lot of time to spend contemplating your life choices.

· DUMB WAYS ᴛᴏ DIE ·

Around 100 people die each year climbing Mont Blanc in the Swiss Alps, thanks in large part to easy access and a gondola that brings woefully unprepared tourists to an altitude of 9,000 feet.

# VIOLENT DEATHS CAN BE SNEAKY

## IN THE ZONE (OF INJURY)

Gunshot victims don't typically die from the bullet itself, but from the force of the bullet's velocity, which expands the zone of injury. If the bullet were implanted instead of shot, it might sit there, completely innocuous. (But that's not a very effective form of self-defense. Or murder.)

## SMOKE GETS IN YOUR EYES (AND LUNGS)

While you may think dying from a fire means being burned to death, it's usually the inhalation injuries that get you. (Noticing a theme here?) Smoke inhalation suffocates a person long before the flames touch skin.

## GORY DETAIL

OFTEN, BOMBING VICTIMS ARE KILLED BY THE IMPACT WAVE FROM THE BLAST—WHICH CAUSES MASSIVE AND UNSURVIVABLE INTERNAL INJURIES—NOT THE PROJECTILES IT CREATES. IN OTHER WORDS, THEIR ORGANS EXPLODE FROM THE FORCE.

## POSITIVELY GLOWING

While the immediate effects of a nuclear explosion are undeniably catastrophic, taking the brunt of the blast might be better than surviving it. Acute radiation syndrome can cause a demise that's anything but quick and painless. It's days to months of skin damage, nausea, vomiting, seizures, infections, and internal bleeding.

## WE'VE GOT A GUSHER

Statistically, your chances of surviving a stabbing are surprisingly high, with survival rates upward of 90 percent if you receive immediate medical attention. Even a lacerated organ can survive. The real trouble is when the knife (or sword, if you're into that kind of thing) nicks an artery, which causes blood to gush out.

## RACISM KILLS

Just existing as a person of color makes you anywhere from 1.6 times to 3.9 times more likely than your white neighbor to die prematurely (depending on where you live). Reasons vary but generally come down to inequities in healthcare, law enforcement, and opportunities, not to mention more overt (read: homicidal) forms of racism.

"IF YOU DIE IN AN ELEVATOR, BE SURE TO PUSH THE 'UP' BUTTON."

—SAM LEVENSON

# WHEN ANIMALS ATTACK

## WATCH OUT FOR HERBIVORES

Everyone's afraid of sharks, which only kill an average of five people a year. But no one thinks twice about sidling up to cattle, which kill an average of twenty-two people a year. Most of those are testosterone-fueled bulls, which are far scarier than sharks.

## WHEN THE CLAWS COME OUT

While Alfred Hitchcock's *The Birds* might seem far-fetched, there's a grain of truth to the terror. The cassowary, a large flightless bird native to Australia and New Guinea that can reach more than six feet tall, earned the title of "most dangerous bird in the world" by gouging people to death with its beak and claws.

> "SOME PEOPLE ARE SO AFRAID TO DIE THAT THEY NEVER BEGIN TO LIVE."
> —HENRY VAN DYKE

## WHAT A BUZZKILL

While a single bee sting is only a minor irritant, a swarm of bees can be lethal, especially to those allergic to their venom. In a particularly bad year, bees can claim up to fifty lives in the United States alone.

## DON'T CROSS A DEER

Bambi may be cute, but deer are one of the deadliest animals in the United States. With over 1.5 million deer-related car accidents and 200 subsequent deaths annually, you'll want to pay more attention to those "deer crossing" signs.

## HUNGRY, HUNGRY HIPPOS

Despite their balloon-like appearance and seemingly lethargic demeanor, hippos are one of the most dangerous animals in Africa, outpacing lions, crocodiles, and cheetahs in the human fatality department. They can sprint up to nineteen miles per hour, and their jaws have a bite force of 1,800 psi, which can easily crush bone.

## • DUMB WAYS TO DIE •

Steve Irwin was an international treasure, but his sudden death by seemingly innocuous stingray is a stark reminder never to underestimate animals— especially when they have sharp, pointy things attached to their bodies. Irwin expected the stingray to retreat when it saw him, but it chose fight over flight that day and ended the Crocodile Hunter's life.

# CHAPTER 5

# DEAD AND BURIED (OR BURNED)

OK, YOU'VE HAD ENOUGH OF THE HISTORY AND THE HEROICS OF DEATH. YOU WANT TO KNOW WHAT HAPPENS ONCE THE MORTICIAN'S GLOVES ARE OFF AND THE MOURNERS HAVE GATHERED. HOW DO YOU GO FROM SKIN AND BONES TO A PILE OF ASH OR A SIX-FOOT-DEEP WORM BUFFET? AND IS IT REALLY SIX FEET? IS IT REALLY ASH? (HINT: NOPE.) GRAB A SHOVEL, AND LET'S DIG IN.

# No-Name Remains

### THE HUMAN LOST AND FOUND

At least 1 percent of all deaths in the United States involve an unclaimed body. That equates to roughly 34,000 unclaimed bodies every year. And if that weren't existentially disconcerting enough, some coroners say those numbers are closer to 3 percent and 100,000.

### ORPHAN CORPSES

Next of kin is under no legal obligation to claim a body. They only have to sign a waiver that they relinquish their rights to it. Who knew there was a worse threat than "Be nice, or I'll put you in the bad nursing home"?

### NURSING HOMES FOR THE AFTERLIFE

Speaking of which, a large number of nursing-home residents are among the unclaimed bodies. Sometimes that's because their records don't include their next of kin, or because their records haven't been updated. But sometimes it's because the next of kin doesn't want to be found.

## DESPERATELY SEEKING KIN

Coroners and funeral-home directors still put a lot of effort into finding *someone* to claim unclaimed bodies. They search through public records, look at police records, hire genealogists and investigators, and place ads in their quest to find family members of the deceased.

. . . . . . . .

## FREEZER BURN

How long coroners search for next of kin depends on available manpower and budget concerns, and there isn't much of either to go around. But it also depends on refrigeration space, and there's even less of that. After all, unclaimed bodies aren't the only ones vying for cold storage.

. . . . . . . .

## DEADEST ELF ON THE SHELF

More often than not, unclaimed bodies end up cremated (for cost efficiency) and either stored on a shelf at the medical examiner's office or dumped in batches in mass graves dedicated to the unknown dead. But if the county has the time and space, they might have a small service and/or bury the ashes in their very own serial-number-marked grave.

"ALWAYS GO TO OTHER PEOPLE'S FUNERALS. OTHERWISE, THEY WON'T COME TO YOURS."

—YOGI BERRA

# The Almost-Final Journey

## FLYING WHILE DEAD

For transport on an airplane, a casket has to be loaded onto an air tray, which is a wooden tray with a cardboard box laid over the top to obscure the casket—because a casket-size cardboard box is not at all conspicuous when being loaded onto a commercial flight in front of a bank of windows.

## THINKING AHEAD

Air trays have an orientation label—a giant stamp that literally says "HEAD." How else would airline staff avoid the embarrassment of loading a body feet first? Everyone knows the feet are supposed to face the door.

## · DUMB WAYS TO DIE ·

If you've ever thought you'd rather stow away than pay ever-more-insane airline prices, think again. Between 1947 and 2012, at least 96 people hid in the wheel compartments of 85 flights. Of those, 73 stowaways died.

## ANOTHER KIND OF JUICE BOX

Air trays typically require bodies to be embalmed because, other-wise, leaks happen, in which case cardboard isn't all that helpful. If you think a casket-size cardboard box is conspicuous, wait until you notice one leaking bodily fluids.

·········

## DYING FOR AN UPGRADE

A body that has to get from A to B by commercial means but has already started to decompose (i.e., probably not embalmed) will be transported in a hermetically sealed steel casket called a "Ziegler." These bad boys are basically zombie proof. No liquid, odor, or—most importantly—infectious disease is getting out.

·········

## CROSS-COUNTRY CADAVER

Alaska and Alabama are the only two states that require that a body be embalmed before crossing state lines, regardless of how it's traveling. (Several other states require it only if the body is traveling with living, breathing, *paying* passengers.)

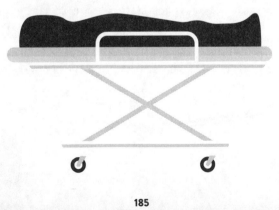

# THE DIRT NAP

## BUSYBODIES

The average cemetery buries 1,250 bodies per acre. For comparison, an acre of dense forest holds about 500 trees and shrubs. So, yeah, that's a lot of bodies for one piece of land.

## DON'T FALL IN

Collapsing caskets and the sinking soil around them can make visiting the dead hazardous to the living, so many cemeteries require a burial vault or grave liner that will keep everything where it's supposed to be.

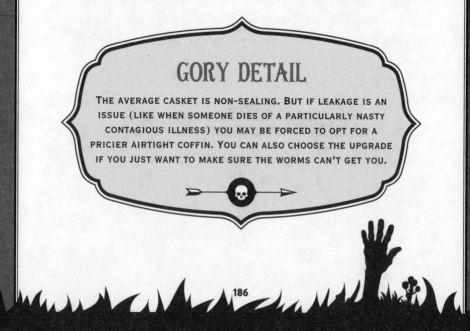

## GORY DETAIL

THE AVERAGE CASKET IS NON-SEALING. BUT IF LEAKAGE IS AN ISSUE (LIKE WHEN SOMEONE DIES OF A PARTICULARLY NASTY CONTAGIOUS ILLNESS) YOU MAY BE FORCED TO OPT FOR A PRICIER AIRTIGHT COFFIN. YOU CAN ALSO CHOOSE THE UPGRADE IF YOU JUST WANT TO MAKE SURE THE WORMS CAN'T GET YOU.

## FAMOUS IN DEATH

Some cemeteries double as tourist destinations. For example, the Père Lachaise Cemetery in Paris is home to more than 70,000 graves, including those of Jim Morrison, Oscar Wilde, and Edith Piaf. That, plus its Gothic, Egyptian, and Renaissance architectural features, makes it a hot spot for visitors.

·········

## NOBODY'S HOME

Another reason (besides visiting expired relations) to seek out a cemetery is ghost hunting. Apps that purport to translate messages from the dead have made the pastime even more popular in recent years. But many hunters agree that cemeteries tend to be less haunted than the average Victorian home because the people who stick around after death tend to do so where they died, not where they're buried.

## · DUMB WAYS ᴛᴏ DIE ·

In 2010, a Russian man decided the best way to get over his fear of dying was to have a buddy bury him in a makeshift grave. He was crushed to death by the weight of the soil. Incredibly, he wasn't the only one—self-burial was a trend in Russia in the early 2000s, thought to bring luck or test endurance.

## THEY'RE HERE!

The indigenous people of North America lived and died here for 20,000 years before Europeans showed up with flags and diseases, which means most of the country is built on native burial grounds. And anyone who's seen *Poltergeist* knows how desecrating cemeteries ends.

........

## PRIME REAL ESTATE

Native Americans tended to bury their dead on hills overlooking beautiful vistas, which were exactly the kinds of views wealthy people wanted when building their homes. One example of this is the Peyton-Randolph house in Williamsburg, Virginia. It was discovered to have been built over a Native American cemetery, and nearly thirty people have died in the house since it was built in 1715. You do the math.

........

## MOVING ON UP

Non-Native cemeteries aren't immune to the pull of progress either. They have been moved to make way for Chicago's Lincoln Park, New Orleans's Superdome, Illinois's Eisenhower Expressway, and Shanghai's Disney Resort, just to name a few.

> "I DO NOT PROPOSE TO BE BURIED UNTIL I AM REALLY DEAD AND IN MY COFFIN."
>
> —DANIEL WEBSTER, ON RUNNING FOR VICE PRESIDENT

# MARKED FOR DEATH

## MORE TO THE STORY

Some gravestones have symbols or codes carved into them that can indicate anything from religious beliefs to fraternal affiliations. You might see a clock-topped elk on the tombstone of an Elk, or an anchor on the grave of a steadfast Christian, or a cherub looking over a child's resting place.

........

## I SPY FOOD POISONING

It's not uncommon to find a stone cookbook opened to the decedent's favorite recipe carved into the top of a tombstone. Of course, you may want to be wary of trying any until you determine what killed the person.

........

## GRAVE DECORATION

Colorful solar-powered and glow-in-the-dark lawn decorations have become popular grave decorations, giving cemeteries an eerie-yet-festive look at night. (You have to admit, neon flamingos are more fun than silk flowers.)

# GOING OUT IN STYLE

## ADD TO CART

You can buy caskets on Amazon as well as from a number of other big-box stores, right alongside your toothpaste and electronics. And they come in a variety of fun colors and finishes, so there's something for everyone. You haven't died until you've seen a metallic-gold or bubblegum-pink casket.

## POST-MORTEM MURALS

Not only can you find pre-decorated caskets covered in everything from military and religious symbols to florals and camo, you can also commission a casket artist to create a custom paint job for you. So you can ensure that your uncle's love of horses is memorialized right along with him.

## MILEAGE MAY VARY

How an unsealed casket (and therefore a body) holds up to time and deterioration depends on the materials it's made out of. Wooden caskets obviously break down faster than metal ones, so if you're going for the "ashes to ashes" effect, wood's the better choice. If you want to be preserved for eternity, metal . . . won't do that. But it'll buy you a few extra years.

# Being Boxed In

### FANTASY COFFINS

In some parts of Africa, particularly Ghana, people make custom caskets called "fantasy coffins" that reflect the personality, occupation, or status of the deceased. For example, a fisherman might be buried in a fish-shaped casket, while a politician might be buried in a book-shaped one.

### TUPPERWARE TOMBS?

In most states, you can be buried in any kind of container you like—especially if you're interred within a burial vault. Always wanted to be buried in wicker, like cheese in a picnic basket? Go for it. The ants are coming either way.

## GORY DETAIL

BODIES STILL GO THROUGH DECOMP IN A CASKET, JUST AT A SLOWER PACE THAN IF THEY ARE EXPOSED TO THE ELEMENTS, MICROBES, AND HUNGRY CRITTERS. BUT, CONTRARY TO WHAT YOU MIGHT THINK, AIRTIGHT CASKETS ACTUALLY INCREASE THE RATE OF DECOMPOSITION. THE SEAL JUST PREVENTS THE RESULTING GASES AND GOO FROM LEACHING INTO SURROUNDING SOIL.

# EXPLODING CASKETS

### DEATH'S SWEET RELEASE

Some sealed caskets come with "burper valves" to release gas buildup so the casket doesn't burst. (Just think of sealed caskets like a pressure cooker, and the stew inside is you.) The valves are "exit only" to retain the worm-deterring features of the casket.

### UNBOXING FOR WEIRDOS

When placing a casket in a mausoleum rather than a grave, caretakers might leave the lid slightly ajar to avoid a mess. So if you notice an unsealed casket, mind your business and be grateful for the expertise of cemetery staff.

## GORY DETAIL

"EXPLODING CASKET SYNDROME" IS A REAL THING. IN THE BATTLE BETWEEN SEALED CASKETS AND THE BUILDING PRESSURE OF DECOMP FLUIDS AND GASES, BIOLOGY SOMETIMES WINS. IT'S NOT QUITE AS DRAMATIC AS IT SOUNDS, THOUGH—INSTEAD OF EXPLODING LIKE A BOMB, THE SEAL BUSTS AND HUMAN GOO SHOOTS OUT OF THE SEAMS. (IT'S NOT DRAMATIC, BUT IT'S STILL GROSS.)

# REDUCE, REUSE, RECYCLE?

## POSTMORTEM POLLUTION

Embalming fluids, metal caskets, and concrete vaults all require significant resources to produce, making traditional burial one of the least eco-friendly disposition methods.

## FOREST FAUX PAS

Making wooden caskets requires cutting down close to 40,000 trees every year in the United States. For comparison, you could build 1,895 houses with that amount of wood. (Or one really big ark, probably.)

## PARKS AND WRECK

Not to mention, cemeteries take up valuable land space and contribute to urban sprawl, reducing natural habitats and green spaces. And which would you rather look at—a lovely park or acres of gravestones?

## A NEW LEASE ON DEATH

In some countries, such as Greece, Germany, and Taiwan, your burial plot isn't necessarily your final resting place. Instead, you rent one for a limited period of time, from as little as three years to as many as twenty years. After that, your remains are exhumed and either cremated or interred in a smaller plot or ossuary.

## DEAD SPACE

Speaking of ossuaries, these skeletal storage spaces are something straight out of *Indiana Jones*. Some are archive boxes made to hold one individual's bones, some are rooms full of the neatly stacked bones of many individuals, and some are entire historical sites that used bones like home decor. (And you can visit them!)

## GORY DETAIL

WHEN BODIES ARE EXHUMED, SOME FAMILIES COME TO WATCH. BUT GRAVEDIGGERS NEVER KNOW WHAT THEY'LL DIG UP. SOME BODIES AREN'T YET FULLY DECOMPOSED, LEAVING A NASTY MESS FOR THEM TO CLEAN UP IN FRONT OF THE DECEDENT'S LOVED ONES. WHATEVER'S LEFT OF THE PERSON GETS UNCEREMONIOUSLY TOSSED INTO A WHEELBARROW FOR EASY TRANSFER TO AN OSSUARY.

### EVERYTHING IN ITS PLACE

A columbarium is the ossuary's neat and tidy cousin. Similar to a mausoleum but without the decaying bodies within smelling distance, it allows families to store cremains in a dedicated reverential space so they don't have to keep Uncle Roger on the mantel.

..........

### SMART STORAGE

In Japan, where land is scarce and expensive, some people opt for alternative burial methods, such as storing cremains in a high-tech columbarium that uses a robotic arm to retrieve the urns and lets mourners pay their respects virtually. (That burial plot you pre-purchased looks pretty boring now, doesn't it?)

.........

### WAIT FOR IT

In tightly packed Hong Kong, a cemetery plot can cost more than a house, and families can wait up to seven years for it (not unlike a spot at a top-tier U.S. preschool). And that waitlist is getting longer as more bodies are exhumed to make room for necessary infrastructure for the living.

"THERE ARE MORE DEAD PEOPLE THAN LIVING, AND THEIR NUMBERS ARE INCREASING. THE LIVING ARE GETTING RARER."
—EUGENE IONESCO

## STACK 'EM UP

Overcrowded UK cemeteries are taking a different tack, using a practice they call "lift and deepen." This is not a breathing exercise at a retreat but a method of exhuming a body and digging the grave deeper to stack another body on top of it.

## CHANGE HAPPENS SLOWLY

Most countries facing grave shortages have turned to cremation to fix the issue. But some predominantly religious countries have not done this because they believe a body is necessary for resurrection. Greece, for example, has only recently built its first and only crematorium.

## PLOT TWIST

Cultural beliefs throw another wrench into the fight for a grave of one's own. Chinese feng shui, for example, dictates that the dead should be buried on mountains facing the sea. The more people cling to those beliefs, the harder it is to implement change that can solve the problem of grave shortages.

# DEAD IN THE WATER

## TOXIC WASTE

More than 4 million gallons of toxic, cancer-causing embalming fluids end up in the ground every year in the United States, which is obviously (not) great for everyone. Not only can it affect the water supply, it can also make its way up the food chain, from worms to birds to living humans.

## BALMY WEATHER

You can cremate an embalmed body, but it means that those toxic chemicals go into the air instead of the ground. And because embalming isn't usually required by law, we're poisoning ourselves voluntarily at this point.

### GORY DETAIL

YOU MAY BE SIPPING ON GREAT-AUNT EDNA WHEN YOU DRINK TAP WATER. ABOUT HALF OF ALL AMERICANS GET THEIR DRINKING SUPPLY FROM UNDERGROUND SOURCES, AND THAT NUMBER'S ONLY GOING TO CLIMB WITH CLIMATE CHANGE MIXING THINGS UP. WHEN BODIES LIQUEFY, ALL THAT GOO GOES INTO THE SURROUNDING SOIL AND, FROM THERE, THE GROUNDWATER.

## POISONING THE WELL

Without the benefit of oxygen to convert it to $CO_2$, methane gas also leaches from the body and into surrounding soil and groundwater. So if that cemetery-adjacent property you've been eyeing comes with well water, best to skip it.

## ARSENIC AND OLD GRAVES

Researchers have recently detected arsenic in the water tables near old burial grounds in places like Iowa and New York that can be traced back to the chemical's use in embalming. But the use of arsenic was outlawed in 1910, which means that it lasts longer than an ultraprocessed snack.

### GORY DETAIL

WHEN CEMETERIES FLOOD, ALL BETS ARE OFF. NOT ONLY DOES THE WATER MORE EFFICIENTLY WASH CHEMICALS AND, RARELY, DISEASES OFF BODIES AND INTO SURROUNDING SYSTEMS, IT CAN ALSO DISLODGE THE BODIES THEMSELVES AND INTRODUCE THEM DIRECTLY TO WATERWAYS.

# "I Don't Need a Box"

### THE SHY WAY TO DIE

Not a fan of the idea of your dead body being ogled? You can choose to skip the viewing and go straight to being cremated; it's called "direct" or "immediate" cremation.

·········

### TO BURY OR BURN

Burial used to be the only way to go, mostly due to religious beliefs that a person needed a body to move on to the next life. But as attitudes changed, interpretations relaxed, and funerals became a much more lucrative (read: expensive) business, cremation began to edge burial out.

·········

### DOWN WITH DECOMPOSING

Approximately 59 percent of dead Americans were cremated in recent years, and that figure continues to rise. That increase might be because people are generally more cost and climate conscious these days, or it might be because the idea of decomposing in a sealed chunk of concrete gives them the ick.

# CREMATION: IT'S NOT WHAT YOU THINK

### HOTTEST TANNING BED ON EARTH

Fire-phobes rejoice! At no point is the body set on fire during cremation. The furnace is heated to up to 2000°F, and it's the extreme heat that reduces the body to gas and bones. Isn't that comforting?

———

### SOME BONES TO PICK

Cremation also doesn't reduce bones to ash. If left undisturbed, the skeleton will remain intact in the cremation chamber, which is politely called a "retort," not an "incinerator," for this reason. If you hear someone calling it an incinerator, you should correct them as haughtily as possible.

———

### DEAD LAST FOR ORIGINALITY

The machine that does the actual cremating is called a "cremator," an almost disappointingly straightforward name and a missed opportunity for something cooler (pun intended).

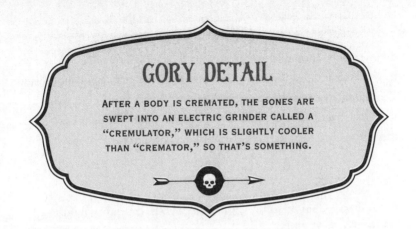

## GORY DETAIL

AFTER A BODY IS CREMATED, THE BONES ARE SWEPT INTO AN ELECTRIC GRINDER CALLED A "CREMULATOR," WHICH IS SLIGHTLY COOLER THAN "CREMATOR," SO THAT'S SOMETHING.

## WHERE'S THE BEEF?

By now, you may be realizing that the term "ashes" is pretty misleading. Cremains (what comes back to you in the urn) are actually just the ground-up bones. Everything else—water, blood, and soft tissue—burns off during cremation.

## PICK UP YOUR LITTER

Cremains (aka ground-up bones) resemble a coarse, gray sand that is not dissimilar to kitty litter, so keep any urns away from cats. That scene in *Meet the Parents* wasn't completely outside the realm of possibility.

"LIFE IS HARD.
AFTER ALL,
IT KILLS YOU."

—KATHARINE
HEPBURN

## ASH FOR DAYS

The average body produces between 3 and 9 pounds of cremains. Age and height factor into that large range, but the real determination is bone density. Theoretically, you could be a wisp of a person and have bones that weigh more than a linebacker's. (That's also one of the reasons the Body Mass Index they use at doctors' offices is nonsense—fat is only one factor in weight.)

## SLOW BURN

It takes two to four hours to fully cremate a body, depending on the temperature of the furnace and the mass of the body, from the time it's loaded into the cremator via conveyor belt to when the bones are swept into the grinder.

## • DUMB WAYS TO DIE •

We've all felt the heat after eating something way too spicy, but one Massachusetts teen actually died from it in 2023 after participating in the "one-chip challenge." That's where people eat a single tortilla chip seasoned with ultra-spicy hot peppers on social media just for the schadenfreude. But with mounting evidence that extreme spice can cause arteries in the brain and heart to constrict, the challenge died with him.

# NOT QUITE A PINE BOX

## A QUICK WARDROBE CHANGE

The kind of casket used in most burials can't go in a cremator because there are too many metal and, frankly, highly toxic components that make burning them a very bad idea. So if you have a viewing, you'll be swapped out from the rental casket and into a cremation-friendly vessel afterward.

........

## STACKABLE STORAGE COFFINS

Most bodies headed for cremation end up in cardboard boxes that look like longer versions of the boxes that hold printer paper, and they're stacked the same way. The only difference is that cremation containers have the kinds of handles every office manager dreams of.

........

## JUST LIKE IKEA

Bodies are placed in wooden or cardboard boxes for cremation not just for easy transfers but also because crematory operators aren't licensed to handle human remains like funeral directors are. The box allows them to move you around like furniture.

# CREMATION PREP

## PATIENT FOR CREMATION

The waiting period between death and cremation differs by state, with some states requiring as little as 24 hours. But most people in the industry recommend waiting up to 72 hours due to the . . . *finality* of the process.

## TICKING HEART BOMB

Pacemakers have to be removed prior to cremation because batteries have a pretty drastic reaction when exposed to intense heat (i.e., BOOM!). The chemicals in a pacemaker's battery can explode with the force of two grams of TNT, which is enough to fire a 16-pound artillery shell at a speed of 60 mph.

## · DUMB WAYS to DIE ·

In 1998, an 82-year-old woman in France mistakenly checked "no" next to "pacemaker" on her husband's intake form before his body was cremated. The crematorium sued her *and* her husband's physician for the ensuing explosion and won £39,000 between them. (No one died, but they could have, so this one gets honorable mention.)

## KEEP YOUR COLLAGEN

Non-metal cosmetic implants and fillers—including those used to prep a body for viewing—dissolve during cremation just like organic material, so they aren't removed beforehand. So your butt could look just as good heading into the furnace as it did in (post-surgical) life.

## PASSING ON USED PACEMAKERS

The European Union and the United States both have regulations forbidding the reuse of implanted medical devices, but the developing world doesn't mind a secondhand pacemaker. Several organizations have popped up to facilitate upcycling the devices from funeral parlors to new recipients.

## AN ARM AND A LEG

Just as they do with pacemakers, some international charities will also take any prosthetic limbs the deceased have to spare. So amputees who are also organ donors can be doubly heroic, saving lives at home and abroad.

........

## DEATH METAL

Metal surgical implants that are removed from the deceased before burial or cremation are often recycled into everyday objects, like cars, traffic signs, and new implants. (Bonus fact: You're going to think of this fact every time you look at a stop sign.)

........

## IMPLANTS ARE OUT

A family can ask for their deceased loved one's implants back, but not many do. Some people have the audacity to ask for the decedent's gold fillings, but no upstanding mortician will honor that request. Some things are just beyond the pale, even for people who work up close and personal with dead bodies.

## GRAVE ROBBING FOR A CAUSE

That's not to say people in the deathcare industry don't occasionally see dollar signs themselves. Once crematoriums realized they could sell leftover metal, regulators got involved to put the kibosh on profiting off of remains. Now, any earnings go to charitable organizations. (But at least the crematorium gets to pick which charities.)

## SCRAP METAL SECRETS

Some crematoriums use a large magnet to remove metal from cremains rather than sifting through by hand. Work smarter, not harder, right?

## HIDDEN GEMS

Precious metals left over after cremation, like those gold fillings, are found by waving a metal detector over the cremains. Per any standard agreement signed by the decedent's family, they become the property of the crematorium and get tossed in the "to go" pile with other scraps to be sold for charity.

"DO NOT TAKE LIFE TOO SERIOUSLY. YOU WILL NEVER GET OUT OF IT ALIVE."

—ELBERT HUBBARD

# LOVE AND CREMATION

## BURN, BOND, AND BEYOND

Despite a couple of exceptions in recent history, loved ones generally can't be cremated together—it's one body per burn. But ashes can be "commin-  gled" after the fact, either by the funeral home or by you at your kitchen table (which should be lined with some kind of tarp if you ever want to eat on it again).

## FREE TO SCATTER

Scattering a loved one's ashes is perfectly legal—mostly. There are some private and public places that prohibit it, but spreading ashes is a widely accepted practice.

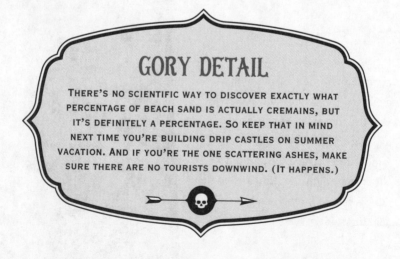

### GORY DETAIL

THERE'S NO SCIENTIFIC WAY TO DISCOVER EXACTLY WHAT PERCENTAGE OF BEACH SAND IS ACTUALLY CREMAINS, BUT IT'S DEFINITELY A PERCENTAGE. SO KEEP THAT IN MIND NEXT TIME YOU'RE BUILDING DRIP CASTLES ON SUMMER VACATION. AND IF YOU'RE THE ONE SCATTERING ASHES, MAKE SURE THERE ARE NO TOURISTS DOWNWIND. (IT HAPPENS.)

# CAUTION: HAZARDOUS MATERIALS

### EARTH-FRIENDLY-ISH

Although mechanized cremation is better than burial for the environment, it's still not great to pump nitrogen oxides, carbon monoxide, and particulate matter into the air. Plus, cremation uses natural gas and electricity to dispose of that ever-growing number of bodies.

### DEADLY EMISSIONS

Cremations in the United States account for about 360,000 metric tons of $CO_2$ emissions each year. That's a drop in the oxygen-starved bucket of our annual average of 6 billion metric tons, but it's still *something*.

### CAUTION TO THE WIND

But it could be worse. In India, Hindu tradition involves cremating the dead on an open-air pyre. RIP to millions of trees, not to mention clean air and rivers.

## TREE HUGGERS REJOICE

Mokshda Green Cremation pyres in India use a metal tray and firewood, saving not only time (it takes a long time to burn a body the old-fashioned way) but also trees. A Mokshda cremation uses only a quarter of the wood of a traditional pyre, and it's estimated that 150,000 Mokshda cremations have saved close to 500,000 trees.

## FINAL SCRUB-DOWN

U.S. crematoriums have scrubbing or filtering systems to neutralize hazardous materials left over from cremation, such as mercury from dental fillings. (And probably also the sticky stuff left over from silicone implants.)

### · DUMB WAYS TO DIE ·

A number of people accidentally pre-cremate themselves each year. The methods range from literally playing with matches to falling asleep while smoking. One woman in Spain doused herself in rosemary alcohol to cool off in the summer heat before fatally lighting a cigarette.

# Think Outside the Urn

## NOT-SO-ETERNAL RESTING PLACES

Being buried six feet under or stuck in a decorative urn and spending eternity on someone's mantel are far from the only options for final disposition. Burial at sea, green burial, biodegradable urns, aquamation, and terramation (aka human composting) are all options that let you leave this world without a trace. Or with a nice plaque, if that's your thing.

## SOLID AS A ROCK

If it's the fragility of the urn full of cremains in your home that freaks you out, you can opt to turn your loved one's ashes into stones that resemble river rocks, which even the most determined pet can't break. (People have tested the theory.)

## ARTS AND CREMAINS

Cremains can also be used to create a variety of things, including jewelry, glass keepsakes, vinyl records, tattoo ink, teddy bears, and marine reefs. If you still want to participate in family game night with your loved ones, you can even opt for an hourglass!

## PAY WHAT YOU WEIGH

Unlike caskets, which are based on total body mass, the size of an urn is based solely on bone mass, which is pretty hard to eyeball. Luckily, manufacturers know an opportunity when they see one—much like the newest kicks, urns come in a variety of sizes per style.

## TRY TO CONTAIN YOURSELF

You can use pretty much anything you want to use as an urn. So if your dream is to spend eternity in a plastic food-storage container, go for it!

## TAKE YOUR TIME

The especially indecisive will be comforted to learn that it's common for people to swap out urns over the years, or even decide on using or scattering their loved one's ashes long after their death. That's one perk of cremation: no ticking clock on the final disposition.

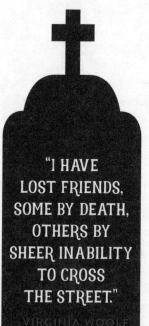

"I HAVE LOST FRIENDS, SOME BY DEATH, OTHERS BY SHEER INABILITY TO CROSS THE STREET."

— VIRGINIA WOOLF

# CREMATION, BUT MAKE IT LIQUID

### BOIL-IN-A-BAG

Alkaline hydrolysis (aka aquamation) is a method of dissolving a human body using a high-pressure chamber filled with roughly 95 percent scalding water and 5 percent alkali solution (aka lye). And it's gaining steam as an accepted method of final disposition.

.........

### HOT POT OF HORROR

In aquamation, the water reaches up to 300°F. For reference, water boils at 212°F—but not this water, thanks to the pressurized chamber. So it's more like a really hot bath than a boiling pot, which should be of some comfort.

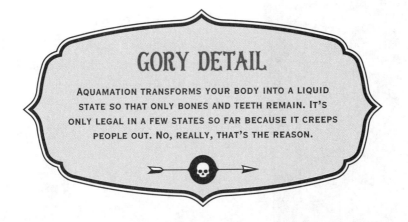

## GORY DETAIL

AQUAMATION TRANSFORMS YOUR BODY INTO A LIQUID STATE SO THAT ONLY BONES AND TEETH REMAIN. IT'S ONLY LEGAL IN A FEW STATES SO FAR BECAUSE IT CREEPS PEOPLE OUT. NO, REALLY, THAT'S THE REASON.

## EXPRESS LANE TO ETERNITY

The aquamation process basically fast-tracks decomp, doing in three to four hours what it takes nature weeks or even years to do. It helps that a scientist calculates the alkalinity based on weight and gender for efficiency— something nature doesn't bother doing.

## PET PROJECT

The technology for aquamation was first patented in England in 1888 and was designed for disposing of animal carcasses. More than 130 years later, the United States is still more open to using the tech for pets than for people despite it being very similar to cremation.

"IT'S FUNNY THE WAY MOST PEOPLE LOVE THE DEAD. ONCE YOU'RE DEAD, YOU'RE MADE FOR LIFE."

—JIMI HENDRIX

## SOUP TO NUTS

Bones aren't the only things left over after alkaline hydrolysis—other inorganic materials, like dental fillings, are left undissolved. But any pathogens and chemicals, including embalming fluid, are safely boiled off.

## NAKED AND (TOO DEAD TO BE) AFRAID

Clothing doesn't break down during aquamation, so the decedent is dressed in a biodegradable shroud. Because modesty is important when you're being turned into human stew.

## DEATH JUICE

The liquid cocktail leftover after aquamation is known as effluent and comprises a sterile mixture of salt, amino acids, soap, and peptides but zero human DNA.

## GORY DETAIL

LIKE ALL OF THE OTHER LOVELY STUFF THAT GOES DOWN THE DRAIN IN FUNERAL HOMES, EFFLUENT GETS RECYCLED AND STERILIZED THROUGH NORMAL WASTEWATER-TREATMENT FACILITIES. YES, INTO YOUR DRINKING WATER (AMONG OTHER THINGS). BUT DON'T WORRY—THEY TEST THE pH FIRST.

## HIPPIES LOVE HYDROLYSIS

Alkaline hydrolysis has about a tenth of the carbon footprint of conventional cremation, making it one of the most eco-friendly, if disgusting, disposition methods available (to a handful of states).

. . . . . . . . .

## BONE DRY

The bones are usually left to dry naturally to keep things green. But if time is more of a factor than carbon footprint, they can be tossed in a mechanical dryer. And once the bones are dry, they get pulverized into "ashes" in a cremulator machine, exactly like they would be after cremation.

. . . . . . . . .

## SUPERIOR SANDS

The pulverized remains from aquamation are whiter, finer, and have 30 percent more volume than traditional cremains. And those in the business consider that a selling point for some reason.

# THE TEA ON BODY COMPOSTING

## GROUNDS FOR CONCERN

Looking for an even greener method of final disposition? You can now have your body composted just like you do with your old coffee grounds—if your state says so. Companies who offer body composting do so in dedicated environmentally controlled facilities. As with aquamation, body composting still freaks out a lot of people even though it's one of the most natural methods out there.

## BY ANY OTHER NAME

The more technical and much more palatable names for human composting are "terramation" or "natural organic reduction."

## SELF-CARE AFTER DEATH

It takes up to twelve weeks to compost a human body, seven of which it spends in a specially designed vessel filled with organic material, like alfalfa and wood chips, tailored to the body's needs. (Sounds almost spa-like, right?)

## FROM THE GROUND UP

Just like with cremation, body composting still requires your bones to be put in a blender (of sorts) to break them down. But they're still full of plant-loving nutrients, so they get added right back to the finished compost.

## THE CIRCLE OF LIFE

Yes, human compost needs to be rotated just like you toss your garden compost pile to make sure that all of it is exposed to the moisture and heat that will help it break down. Instead of rake or a shovel, they use a really big crank to rotate the terramation vessel.

## SORRY, CSI

Once the body is completely composted, no human DNA remains. You are now one with the soil, which makes this a really eco-friendly option but also a great way to ensure the deceased can't be implicated in past crimes. (Again, not advice.)

........

## OLD MACDONALD HAD A MORGUE

The idea for human composting came from a farming practice called "mortality composting," an emergency response to mass animal deaths (think avian flu). But instead of being tossed with old produce in a silo, you get that personal touch.

........

## AL OUT OF LUCK

You can't be composted if you've been embalmed. So Alabama residents are out of luck when it comes to terramation because it's not yet legal in their state, and they require bodies to be embalmed to cross state lines.

"I'VE LOOKED THAT OLD SCOUNDREL DEATH IN THE EYES MANY TIMES, BUT THIS TIME I THINK HE HAS ME ON THE ROPES."

—DOUGLAS MACARTHUR

## BACK TO THE EARTH

Each body creates about 1 cubic yard of nutrient-dense compost. (That's more than 1,000 pounds of compost, if metric measurements aren't your thing.) It can be used like any other compost to enrich soil for plant growth.

........

## A LESS GASSY WAY TO GO

Not only is the resulting compost good for the environment, but the process itself is, too. Terramation releases between .84 and 1.4 metric tons of carbon dioxide *less* than cremation and burial *per body*.

........

## UNDEAD ECO-WARRIOR

If you choose human composting as your disposition method, you can opt to donate your resulting body compost to conservation organizations to help with efforts like reforestation.

# GREEN IS THE NEW BLACK

## A GRAVE CONCERN

Green burial (being buried directly in the soil or in a biodegradable casket) has the lowest carbon footprint of any of the disposition methods. But because it's still so novel—despite being closer to how people were laid to rest for literal millennia before the deathcare industry existed—it can come with a hefty price tag.

........

## IT'S EASY BEING GREEN

There are more than 150 "green cemeteries" in the United States that allow more natural burials. They need their own designation because the laws that regulate cemeteries were set up for more standardized, commercial disposition and don't permit things like native landscaping. The States take lawn-mowing seriously.

## · DUMB WAYS TO DIE ·

Trying to live and die with less of a carbon footprint isn't a bad thing—unless you accidentally die as a result of it. One Colorado family died of malnutrition and hypothermia while trying to live off the grid. Most people would have given up at the first hunger pang, but this trio was nothing if not tenacious. Dead, but tenacious.

## THE CADILLAC OF CARDBOARD

Crematoriums aren't the only place for cardboard caskets. Showier versions come dressed up with eco-friendly liners and better load-bearing handles for use in green burial. It's a nice compromise between a basic shroud and a casket that will outlast all of the Botox in Beverly Hills.

.........

### IT DOUBLES AS A PLANTER!

Some companies offer composting caskets that they fill with organic material to help the deceased decompose into the earth without all the fuss of being tossed and processed at a facility first.

## GORY DETAIL

DURING A NATURAL, OR GREEN, BURIAL, THE BODY IS BURIED 3 TO 4 FEET UNDERGROUND RATHER THAN THE TRADITIONAL 6 FEET NEEDED TO ACCOMMODATE A CASKET AND VAULT. THIS STILL PROVIDES THE ALL-IMPORTANT 18- TO 24-INCH "SMELL BARRIER" TO ENSURE THAT ANIMALS DON'T CATCH THE SCENT OF YOUR REMAINS AND GO SCAVENGING.

# BLOOM WHERE YOU'RE PLANTED

### KILLER CREMAINS

The growing number of people who want to "become a tree" (or other plant) when they die might be devastated to learn that cremains aren't actually good for plants—they're extremely high in alkalinity and concentrated minerals, like calcium. So scattering Grandpa Joe in the garden will probably send his beloved roses to the other side with him.

### PUTTING DOWN ROOTS

Bio-urns trade on the idea of people "becoming" plants because they are biodegradable urns that hold a plant. But it's their proprietary pH-balancing chemical additive that makes cremains safe for those plants. The cremains themselves don't help things along.

### BRANCHING OUT

You can be cremated and spread beneath a tree, but you can't be buried under one. To protect a tree's root system, a body must be buried at least 4 feet away from it. (But anyone who's seen tree roots break through a sidewalk probably doesn't want to think about what happens to a body that gets in their way.)

## DREAM SMALLER

If you don't mind "becoming" a small shrub or perennial flower instead of a tree, green burial is an option because your body won't disturb their shallow root systems. You can have someone landscape right over your grave.

## FINDING BALANCE

The closest you can get to becoming a tree is through terramation. The pH of a composted body rings in between 6.5 and 7, which is perfect for plants. And as nutrient-rich compost, your remains will actually nurture any memorial greenery rather than slowly poisoning it.

## WORTH A TRY

"LIFE IS HARD. THEN YOU DIE. THEN THEY THROW DIRT IN YOUR FACE. THEN THE WORMS EAT YOU. BE GRATEFUL IT HAPPENS IN THAT ORDER."

—DAVID GERROLD

At least one company is trying to one-up terramation by creating burial pods that can be "planted" like seeds. The deceased is placed inside in the fetal position (pre- or post-rigor). It may be poetic, but, as of yet, it's still more science fiction than science.

## 'SHROOMING

In 2019, actor Luke Perry caused one last stir by being buried in a zero-waste mushroom suit. This is a onesie made from genetically engineered mushrooms that help speed up decomposition by eating human flesh. And it's available to the public at large for a very reasonable $1,500—roughly the price of a mid-range casket.

........

## FUTURE-MINDED FUNERAL HOMES

Feeding the greenery with your dismembered corpse isn't the only way to combat rampant deathcare emissions. Some funeral homes are going green by investing in renewable energy and planting trees for each body they bury. Is it usually nothing more than a marketing technique? Sure. But every tree counts.

## · DUMB WAYS ᴛᴏ DIE ·

A favorite among the green-minded is the humble coconut. This is a fruit so versatile that it not only sustains life but also commits murder. Roughly 150 people worldwide die each year from being hit by falling coconuts.

# CHAPTER 6

# The Business of Death

FROM FORENSICS AND BODY FARMS TO PHARMACEUTICALS AND FUNERALS, DYING AND DEATHCARE ARE BIG BUSINESS. THIS FINAL CHAPTER ABOUT THE FINAL CHAPTER DETAILS HOW DEATH IS ALL IN A DAY'S WORK—AND EQUALS A FAT PAYCHECK—IN A SOCIETY WHERE CAPITALISM IS KING. ARMED WITH INSIDER INFO ON LAWS, PRICING, AND OVERSIGHT, YOU MAY EVEN MEET THE GRIM REAPER WITH YOUR WALLET INTACT.

# IT'S NOT PERSONAL, IT'S BUSINESS

## IT'S FUN TO WORK AT THE N-F-D-A!

Organizations like the International Cemetery, Cremation and Funeral Association (ICCFA) and National Funeral Directors Association (NFDA) set guidelines for the deathcare industry, lest any funeral-home owners decide to go rogue.

## AWFULLY ENTREPRENEURIAL

Historians credit the nineteenth century with the birth of the deathcare industry. That's when cities began to expand and coffin makers saw dollar signs in offering up extra services, like burial clothes, flowers, body prep, and transportation.

## GORY DETAIL

TODAY, THE FUNERAL BUSINESS IN THE UNITED STATES IS A $20 BILLION-A-YEAR INDUSTRY. THERE'S NOTHING PARTICULARLY GORY ABOUT THIS FACT IN THE TRADITIONAL SENSE, BUT ONCE YOU LEARN HOW MUCH OF THAT FIGURE COMES FROM PREYING ON THE BEREAVED, YOU'LL FIND IT GRUESOME.

## MISERY LOVES COMPANY

The global deathcare market was valued at $134 billion in 2022 and is expected to grow to more than $150 billion by 2028. So if your wallet's a little light after preplanning your funeral, at least you're not alone!

.........

## AN EMBARASSMENT OF RICHES

The fines levied against excessively flashy funerals in Colonial America paved the way for later laws reining in funerary costs. For example, the Massachusetts Bay Province enacted a law in 1761 prohibiting such extravagances as scarves, gloves, wine, rum, and rings from being gifted at funerals.

.........

## FTC = FIGHTING THEM CREEPS

So many funeral homes were engaging in shady practices, like forcing people to add expensive and unnecessary options, that the Federal Trade Commission (FTC) had to get involved. They created the Funeral Rule, which requires funeral homes to be up-front about pricing.

"MY FATHER WAS FROM ABERDEEN, AND A MORE GENEROUS MAN YOU COULDN'T WISH TO MEET. I HAVE A GOLD WATCH THAT BELONGED TO HIM. HE SOLD IT TO ME ON HIS DEATHBED. I WROTE HIM A CHEQUE FOR IT, POST-DATED, OF COURSE."

—BUDDY HACKETT

## KEEP CALM AND EMBALM ON (OR NOT)

Embalming isn't actually necessary to preserve most bodies—modern refrigeration techniques are all you really need to help the deceased make it to the funeral intact. But it's become so common in the United States that people assume it's required. And, like pharmaceutical companies pushing particular drugs, some unscrupulous funeral homes will actively profit off that misconception.

## · DUMB WAYS TO DIE ·

Running a business doesn't always mean you make smart decisions. Segway owner Jimi Heselden rode his own creation off a cliff while gliding around his estate in a tragic 2010 accident.

## NO PRESERVATIVES

Embalming is common in places like North America, Great Britain, New Zealand, and Australia, but not so much in areas like Europe. There, they favor a slower pace of life but a much quicker and less showy final disposition. (And, generally, fewer chemicals in their soil.)

.........

## TRAVEL CAN BE DRAINING

Live passengers aren't the only ones who have to empty their liquids before a flight. Some states require a body be embalmed if it's crossing state lines or flying commercial (for both sticky and odiferous reasons).

.........

## THE ROYAL TREATMENT

Conspiracy theorists believed Diana, Princess of Wales, was embalmed to destroy evidence of a secret pregnancy. But the real and perfectly boring reasons were the lengthy journey to her grave and the warm chapel where her funeral was held.

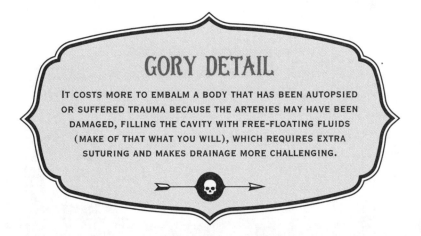

## GORY DETAIL

IT COSTS MORE TO EMBALM A BODY THAT HAS BEEN AUTOPSIED OR SUFFERED TRAUMA BECAUSE THE ARTERIES MAY HAVE BEEN DAMAGED, FILLING THE CAVITY WITH FREE-FLOATING FLUIDS (MAKE OF THAT WHAT YOU WILL), WHICH REQUIRES EXTRA SUTURING AND MAKES DRAINAGE MORE CHALLENGING.

# NICKEL-AND-DIMING DEATH

## POST-MORTEM PRICE CONTROL

Funerals are pricey, even without the used-car-salesmen-style funeral homes dragging the good name of ethical morticians through the mud. But thanks to the FTC's Funeral Rule, every funeral home is required to have and provide you with a set price list up front.

## READ THE FINE PRINT

In addition to the price list, funeral homes will provide you (or your next of kin, should you not be the preplanning type) with a contract listing every possible option so you can choose what you want and decline what you don't. Once you sign on the dotted line, there shouldn't be any unexpected expenses.

## SORRY FOR YOUR LOSS

The median cost of a funeral in the United States is $7,000—and that's if you opt for cremation. Burial will run you another $1,000 to $2,000, or possibly even more if you spring for extras like a burial vault or a sealed casket. (More on that particular racket to come.)

## NOT DIGGING THE PRICE

Burial is more expensive than cremation because it includes more post-mortem accoutrements: the cemetery plot, grave opening (hole digging), grave closing (hole filling), headstone or vault, and the physical lowering of the casket, with all its related mechanics.

## A ROOM WITH A VIEW

The cost of burial doesn't always include the cost of a burial plot, which can shake out to anywhere from $1,000 to $4,000, depending on whether you had your heart set on a crowded city graveyard or a hill overlooking the countryside.

### · DUMB WAYS ᴛᴏ DIE ·

You might think that being crushed to death by currency is the stuff of cartoons and heist movies. But Hrand Arakelian would tell you otherwise—if he hadn't been flattened by several 25-pound boxes of quarters in 1986 after having to hit the brakes suddenly while driving a bank truck.

## A HOLE IN THE WALL

Burial plots are a bargain compared to purchasing a crypt in a public mausoleum, which averages $7,000 to $8,000 in the United States. Even a 9-inch cremation niche—a literal hole in the wall—costs between $750 and $2,800.

### GORY DETAIL

NO ONE WANTS TO PROFIT OFF THE DEATH OF A CHILD, AND THAT INCLUDES EVEN THE MOST HARDENED MORTICIANS. THEY CAN HANDLE THE MOST GRUESOME DEATHS WITHOUT BREAKING A SWEAT, BUT PREPARING A CHILD WEIGHS HEAVILY ON THEM. MANY WILL PROVIDE SERVICES FOR STILLBORN INFANTS AND YOUNG BABIES AT COST.

### HEY, GAS IS EXPENSIVE

Both mortuaries and crematoriums charge a per-mile transfer fee for picking up a body. But don't be tempted to park a body at the morgue. Much like airport garages, they'll charge you somewhere between $35 and $100 per day.

"THE ONLY DIFFERENCE BETWEEN DEATH AND TAXES IS THAT DEATH DOESN'T GET WORSE EVERY TIME CONGRESS MEETS."

—WILL ROGERS

# DYING TO SAVE SOME DOUGH

## JUST SAY NO TO UPSELLS

Planning ahead is the best way to save money on a funeral and not get taken to the cleaners (a more disturbing thought when the cleaner is a guy with an embalming trocar). If you have all your loved one's wishes mapped out in advance, it's harder to fall prey to lines like, "Doesn't your mother *deserve* the Platinum Package?"

## SERVING OUR SERVICE MEMBERS

In death as in life, it never hurts to ask for a military discount. Veterans discharged with honors can be buried for free at a Veterans Affairs National Cemetery. The grave, vault, opening, closing, and marker are all included—quite the package deal!

## SHOP AROUND (SERIOUSLY)

Best Buy isn't the only business with a price-match guarantee. Funeral directors are more willing than you might think to match or beat a competitor's offers, and that FTC Funeral Rule makes it easy to compare price lists.

# DIY FUNERAL PREP

## BARGAIN SHOPPING ENCOURAGED

Per the FTC, you don't have to buy what your funeral home is selling. You can get an urn or casket from a third-party seller, and the funeral home legally has to use it. They may not be happy about it, but they have to use it.

## YOU GET WHAT YOU PAY FOR

It's not greed that makes morticians blanch at cheap funerary products. It's that you get what you pay for. Morticians will do what they can to make your loved one look great regardless of the ill-fitting interior of a big-box-store casket, but it makes their lives harder.

## THE YOUTUBE MORTICIAN

If you think you can do it better yourself, you're welcome to try. You can legally prepare, care for, and view the deceased in your own home—no funeral home, mortician, or fee schedule required. (Though you'll still need transport and disposition services.)

# CASKETS ARE LIKE CARS

## A DEALER'S A DEALER

People tend to buy the mid-priced option of the first three caskets they see, so funeral homes tend to show them only the most expensive options. Funny how that works! They'll even keep the lower-priced caskets out of the showroom, knowing most people won't buy something sight unseen.

## LARGER THAN LIFE

Standard caskets can hold up to 300 pounds. If the deceased weighs more than that, you can expect an upcharge for a big-and-tall-style casket that has a weight capacity of 500 pounds.

## GORY DETAIL

SEALED CASKETS ARE MORE EXPENSIVE THAN UNSEALED ONES, WHICH MEANS A FUNERAL DIRECTOR LOOKING TO PAD THEIR PROFITS IS MORE LIKELY TO PUSH SEALED CASKETS AS A WAY TO BETTER PRESERVE A CUSTOMER'S LOVED ONE. BUT, IF YOU'VE READ CHAPTER 5, YOU KNOW THAT COULDN'T BE FURTHER FROM THE TRUTH. SEALED CASKETS HAVE A TENDENCY TO SPEED DECOMP AND EXPLODE DUE A BUILDUP OF GASES. AT LEAST THE FUNERAL RULE FORBIDS FUNERAL DIRECTORS FROM CLAIMING THAT CASKETS OR SPECIAL CASKET FEATURES CAN PRESERVE A BODY FOREVER.

# MOVING ON UP (AND OUT)

### CASKET FAKE OUT

If you choose cremation but still want a viewing, you can rent a casket for a very reasonable $750—minimum. Hot tip: People generally aren't looking at the casket when there's a dead body in the room. Skip the bells and whistles.

### LIKE UNCOMFORTABLE SEATS AT A RESTAURANT

Burial plots may be expensive in the United States, but at least you're getting your money's worth. In countries like Greece, where burial space is at a premium, you rent plots for three years. You can rent for longer, but each extra year is purposely prohibitively expensive to deter lingering.

### BURIAL (AND UN-BURIAL)

Once your lease is up in Greece, you have to pay to have the decedent's bones exhumed and moved to an ossuary—for which you also have to pay rent. (Worse still is the trauma tax of seeing your loved one's bones.)

# GREEN IS THE NEW BLACK

## AN ENVIRONMENTAL GOLD STAR

The National Funeral Directors Association has a Green Funeral Practices™ certificate program. It recognizes funeral homes that have adopted and implemented ethical and sustainable green funeral and business practices, helping climate-conscious customers sort the nutrient-dense compost from the trash, so to speak.

## THE PERKS OF COMPOSTING

Body composting costs between $5,000 and $7,000, which is slightly better than the cost of cremation or traditional burial. The knowledge that your decomposed body is making plants bloom a little bigger: priceless.

"I'M RATHER RELAXED ABOUT DEATH. FROM QUITE AN EARLY AGE, I'VE REGARDED IT AS PART OF THE DEAL, THE UNWRITTEN GUARANTEE THAT COMES WITH YOUR BIRTH CERTIFICATE."

—DOUG BENSON

## SOFTWOODS FOR THE WIN

Green burial costs the same as traditional burial (both require holes to be dug, filled, and marked), but biodegradable caskets are far less expensive because they forego all of the hardwoods, metals, and luxe-looking details (i.e., a funeral home's bread and butter).

## CUE THE WATERWORKS

Aquamation costs between $2,000 and $3,300, which is an eco-friendly bargain compared with traditional burial. But it's even more impressive when you find out that funeral homes will pay anywhere from $150,000 to $400,000 for an alkaline hydrolysis machine, or resomator, which is the machine used to perform aquamation.

## HIDDEN AGENDA

Part of the reason aquamation isn't legal in all fifty states is because religious organizations and casket-makers have lobbied against it, for totally legitimate and not at all self-serving reasons.

## · DUMB WAYS TO DIE ·

Famous Greek Olympian Milo of Croton learned the hard way not to mess with Mother Nature when he decided to test his strength by trying to split a log with his bare hands. Legend has it that his fingers got stuck in the wood, and wolves took advantage of his predicament.

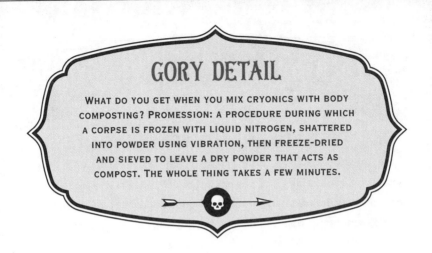

## GORY DETAIL

WHAT DO YOU GET WHEN YOU MIX CRYONICS WITH BODY COMPOSTING? PROMESSION: A PROCEDURE DURING WHICH A CORPSE IS FROZEN WITH LIQUID NITROGEN, SHATTERED INTO POWDER USING VIBRATION, THEN FREEZE-DRIED AND SIEVED TO LEAVE A DRY POWDER THAT ACTS AS COMPOST. THE WHOLE THING TAKES A FEW MINUTES.

## NO ASSEMBLY REQUIRED

The concept of promession came from Swedish biologist Susanne Wiigh-Mäsak, because only the Swedes could come up with such a hardcore disposition method. Wiigh-Mäsak got the name of the procedure from the Italian word for promise (*promessa*), which is oddly sweet for something so disturbing.

## PERMISSION TO PROMESS (DENIED)

Sadly, for those in search of eco-friendly disposition methods and sci-fi fans alike, promession is still considered experimental and is not offered to the public. Yet.

# EXPERTS IN DEATH AND DYING

## LIKE A DEATH COACH

Plenty of businesses have monetized dying, but some have more wholesome intentions. Similar to birthing doulas, death doulas provide the ultimate transition assistance—physical, emotional, and spiritual support and guidance for people and their families during the dying process.

## A FORWARD THINKER

The term "death doula" started with Henry Fersko-Weiss, a social worker who practices what he preaches. He founded the International End of Life Doula Association (INELDA) in 2015.

## · DUMB WAYS TO DIE ·

There's nothing wrong with taking a holistic approach to life and death, but the untimely demise of Basil Brown in 1974 makes a case for enjoying all things in moderation. He succumbed to cirrhosis of the liver from overindulging . . . in carrot juice.

## MAKE YOUR FUNERAL DREAMS A REALITY

Death doulas can help you articulate your wishes for medical care, final arrangements, and memorial services, which makes theirs an especially handy service for those with overbearing family members. (If you can't get what you want when you're dying, when can you?)

## ALL-PURPOSE ADVOCATES

Not only do death doulas help lighten the load of the dying, they also help the living process their grief and get through the final arrangements with their sanity and bank accounts intact. (As much as is humanly possible, anyway.)

## FIVE-STAR SERVICE

Training to become a death doula typically involves coursework, workshops, and practical experience. But there's no governing requirements, so vet your death doula as carefully as you do your restaurants (i.e., look for reviews and recommendations).

# CARDS AND BODIES ON THE TABLE

## THE UPSIDE OF BUREAUCRACY

Death certificates, which are required for both burial and cremation, have to be jointly signed by a medical certifier (a physician, coroner, or medical examiner) and a licensed funeral director. That certainly cuts down on the odds of being buried or burned alive.

## IT NEVER HURTS TO CHECK

Not every body gets autopsied, but the ones that do aren't always the victims of sinister motives (as TV dramas and true-crime podcasts would have you believe). There are plenty of innocuous reasons to perform an autopsy, like determining whether it was genetics or a lifetime of bacon cheeseburgers that did Grandpa Pete in.

## · DUMB WAYS to DIE ·

Sometimes, business interests are what get you killed (and not just in mafia- and gambling-related incidents). Sources claim that approximately 2,500 left-handed people die each year from using products designed for right-handed people.

## THE COMFORTS OF CONFIRMATION

In some cases, a condition that a person had in life can only be diagnosed after they die. For instance, doctors can learn for certain that someone had Alzheimer's disease only after they examine the brain in an autopsy. It's up to the family to decide whether to allow it.

.........

## CAN I SEE YOUR LICENSE?

In twenty states and the District of Columbia, a medical examiner—a medical doctor who specializes in the study of disease and injury, also called a forensic pathologist—has to do the autopsy. In the other states, coroners can do them and have to be trained in death investigation, but they are not required to have any medical training, let alone an MD.

.........

## STATE-MANDATED MYSTERY SOLVERS

Twenty-seven states require an autopsy if the cause of death is suspected to be from a public health threat (think outbreak-level flu or suspiciously sickening chicken salad). This is where science meets detective work, and coroners learn which packaged foods to avoid.

> "ONE MUST NEVER SET UP A MURDER. THEY MUST HAPPEN UNEXPECTEDLY, AS IN LIFE."
>
> —ALFRED HITCHCOCK

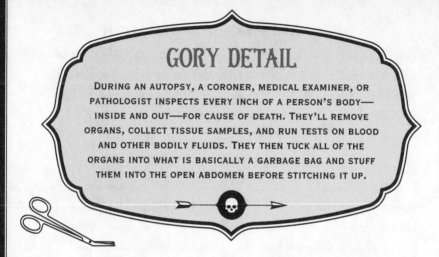

## GORY DETAIL

DURING AN AUTOPSY, A CORONER, MEDICAL EXAMINER, OR PATHOLOGIST INSPECTS EVERY INCH OF A PERSON'S BODY— INSIDE AND OUT—FOR CAUSE OF DEATH. THEY'LL REMOVE ORGANS, COLLECT TISSUE SAMPLES, AND RUN TESTS ON BLOOD AND OTHER BODILY FLUIDS. THEY THEN TUCK ALL OF THE ORGANS INTO WHAT IS BASICALLY A GARBAGE BAG AND STUFF THEM INTO THE OPEN ABDOMEN BEFORE STITCHING IT UP.

## CUTTING BACK ON CUTTING PEOPLE OPEN

Autopsies used to be performed on half of all Americans. In fact, hospitals used to perform them as a matter of course. But budget cuts have hit hard in recent years, and doctors are sick of being second-guessed. Now, fewer than 10 percent of deaths warrant an autopsy.

## YOU CAN ALWAYS COUNT ON CAPITALISM

Although the local (and sometimes federal) government handles autopsies of suspicious deaths, they don't always agree with family members about what constitutes a suspicious death.
In these instances, families can avail themselves of private pathologists—for a fee, of course.

## CONCIERGE-LEVEL SERVICE

A private autopsy will cost you between $3,000 and $5,000—a number that keeps going up as the frequency of public autopsies go down. But you do get more bang for your buck, walking away with a more comprehensive evaluation than you would likely get from a government employee who only cares about cause of death.

## PRIVATE AUTOPSIES SAVE LIVES

If a family member drops dead unexpectedly, but the death isn't ruled as suspicious, you may never know what caused it. But knowing could save your life if the cause is a genetic condition that you share with the deceased.

### · DUMB WAYS TO DIE ·

Despite rumors to the contrary, you are allowed to die in Longyearbyen, Svalbard. But residents are required to move to the mainland once they become elderly or sick (i.e., ready to die), not only because there's little healthcare infrastructure on this Norwegian archipelago deep inside the Arctic Circle but also because the ground is so cold there that bodies barely decompose. Dying while infectious in a place where infections can't die: not great.

# REFRIGERATION FOR THE WIN

## THAT'S NOT WHAT THAT FRIDGE IS FOR

Despite what you see on TV, you won't actually catch a coroner eating a sandwich next to a dead body. Mortuaries have stricter cleanliness standards than most hospitals. This isn't just to keep the deceased dignified, but also to prevent staff from hosting unwanted parties of microorganisms.

## THE COLD NEVER BOTHERED THEM ANYWAY

Before modern refrigeration, preserving a body for a funeral was a race against time. Now, morticians can use colder temperatures to preserve a body for up to four weeks, and in better shape than embalming would in the same time frame.

## FROZEN IN TIME

Keeping a body on ice isn't just handy for funeral homes. It also allows researchers and coroners alike to study bodies and diseases at their leisure, without the pressure of a ticking biological clock.

"THE POLICE LIKE TO BELIEVE MURDERS ARE COMMITTED BY THOSE WE KNOW AND LOVE, AND MOST OF THE TIME THEY'RE RIGHT—A CHILLING THOUGHT WHEN YOU SIT DOWN TO DINNER WITH A FAMILY OF FIVE."

—SUE GRAFTON

# LAW & ORDER: RIP

### LIKE GETTING AN EXTENSION ON A PAPER

In the world of police work, refrigeration has been a game-changer. Gone are the days of needing a speedy autopsy before nature takes its course. Now, detectives can return to the body to double-check details and collect new evidence while they investigate complex crimes.

### CHEMICALS CATCH MURDERERS

To be as precise as possible in calculating time of death (TOD)—a pretty important factor in catching the bad guy during a criminal investigation—

 forensic scientists study the 400 chemicals present in the varying stages of decomposition. Taking variables like temperature, humidity, and access to oxygen into account, they can use the body's level of decomp to work backward to TOD.

### POINT AND SHOOT

Scientists have discovered that thirty of those chemicals, when found together, provide evidence that hidden remains are nearby. And they've developed a handheld instrument that can detect them, which is better than anything *CSI* had.

## DNA IS FOREVER

Thanks to their rigid structure, bones hold viable DNA
after death, making them super handy to have around when
attempting to solve their owner's murder. And for cloning your
childhood pet, probably.

## TAKING A BITE OUT OF CRIME

In addition to DNA, forensic scientists can identify bodies by tooth
morphology, variations in shape and size, restorations, pathologies,
missing teeth, wear patterns, crowding of the teeth, color and position of a
tooth, rotations, and dental anomalies.

# DYING ᶠᵒʳ ᵃ GOOD CAUSE

## GREAT RETURN ON INVESTMENT

As you learned in Chapter 2, one organ donor can save eight lives. You can donate your kidneys, liver, lungs, heart, pancreas, intestines, skin, and corneas, all of which will be transported to wherever they're needed across the country. (In case you felt bad about not traveling enough in life.)

## TEACHING WITHOUT A LICENSE

If you've always wanted to go to medical school but didn't have the attention span for seven-plus years of studying, you can donate your body to science. Medical students will practice procedures on your corpse so they don't accidentally create another one when they start practicing medicine for real.

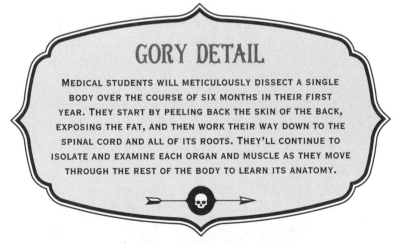

### GORY DETAIL

MEDICAL STUDENTS WILL METICULOUSLY DISSECT A SINGLE BODY OVER THE COURSE OF SIX MONTHS IN THEIR FIRST YEAR. THEY START BY PEELING BACK THE SKIN OF THE BACK, EXPOSING THE FAT, AND THEN WORK THEIR WAY DOWN TO THE SPINAL CORD AND ALL OF ITS ROOTS. THEY'LL CONTINUE TO ISOLATE AND EXAMINE EACH ORGAN AND MUSCLE AS THEY MOVE THROUGH THE REST OF THE BODY TO LEARN ITS ANATOMY.

## A GRATITUDE PRACTICE, IF YOU WILL

Med students often hold "gratitude ceremonies" to say a respectful goodbye to their cadavers at the end of the exercise and thank them for everything the students learned from them.

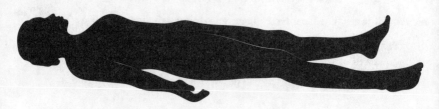

## MAKE YOURSELF USEFUL

Instead of growing crops, body farms are growing microbes . . . on donated bodies strewn about an open lot so researchers can study their decomposition under a variety of factors. It's like body composting, but in a way that's creepier yet more educational.

## MAN'S BEST FRIEND NEEDS YOUR FEMUR

Cadaver dogs are not just man's best friend; they're also detectives' best colleagues. They're trained to follow their noses to dead bodies using donated cadavers so they can help solve murders and reunite loved ones. And they work for treats, not cash, making them the most cost-effective investigators around.

# MORE MORBID MONEY GRABS

## EVERY OBITUARY IS AN OPPORTUNITY

Death means big business for anyone who deals in estate sales, from lawyers, appraisers, and organizers to treasure hunters, casual shoppers, and antique stores. Some people will even browse obituaries like yard-sale notices.

*In loving memory*

..........

## FINAL DESTINATIONS

Fatally ill people often have to travel to find compassionate care. Suicide tourism, as it's called, sees them journey to states like New Jersey and Oregon and countries like Switzerland, where assisted dying is both legal and dignified.

### · DUMB WAYS TO DIE ·

Alfred Rouse faked his demise in 1930 to avoid paying child support for several illegitimate children. The kicker is that, to carry out this ruse, he bludgeoned a hitchhiker to death and then put the man's body in his own burning car. Rouse was obviously hanged for murder.

# DEATH IS GREAT FOR TOURISM

## GOING DARK ON VACATION

Cemeteries aren't the only things bringing the crowds (and the bucks). Dark tourism is a booming industry, attracting inquisitive visitors and history buffs to the sites of natural disasters, grisly murders, mass suicides, and many other places tragic and macabre.

## DEATH WITH A SIDE OF GELATO

One spot that hides its dark history well in the midst of art, architecture, and culture is Rome's Colosseum. An estimated 400,000 people—mostly the poor and marginalized—and 1 million animals died within its walls just for funsies.

## A WIDE VARIETY OF TOURS

Although plenty of these sites cater to the morbidly curious, like drug lord Pablo Escobar's compound (a tour of which may be given by one of his most merciless hitmen!), others serve to honor history and soberly remind us of humanity's greatest horrors. One of those is Germany's Holocaust Memorial and Museum Auschwitz-Birkenau, which has served more than 25 million visitors. Another is the 9/11 Museum and Memorial in New York City, which attracts an average of 9,000 visitors each day.

## A VIEW OF TRAGEDY

Pompeii is the site of one of the most tragic volcano-related disasters in history, claiming at least 2,000 lives in the city alone. So naturally, it's a hot spot for tourism, with 2.5 million visitors each year. They get to see plaster casts of dead bodies as well as the remains of the residents' homes and lives.

........

## AN EXPLOSIVELY GOOD TIME

Chernobyl, the site of the 1986 nuclear power-plant explosion, is only a few decades into the 20,000 years scientists say it will need to recover from the radiation's effects. But that doesn't stop tens of thousands of people going to see the ghostly Exclusion Zone, with its eerie abandoned Ferris wheel.

## GORY DETAIL

THE KHMER ROUGE REGIME MURDERED MORE THAN 1 MILLION POLITICAL PRISONERS IN CAMBODIA BETWEEN 1974 AND 1979. TODAY, YOU CAN VIEW THE SKULLS OF 8,000 VICTIMS EXHUMED FROM MASS GRAVES KNOWN AS "THE KILLING FIELDS" AND EVER-SO-NICELY DISPLAYED BEHIND GLASS IN THE CHOEUNG EK MEMORIAL STUPA.

# The World Is One Big Haunted House

## REACH OUT AND TOUCH SOMEONE

Over 1.5 million people visit San Francisco's Alcatraz prison, now a national park, for its dark history, scenic vistas, and well-advertised haunting activity. You can even book a ghost tour and have a chance to feel the wrath of such ruthless criminals as Whitey Bulger firsthand.

## GHOSTS, WITCHES, AND HISTORY—OH MY!

Salem, Massachusetts, offers a double draw for its 1 million annual visitors—ghosts *and* witches. And thanks to the poor treatment of the latter, more of the former may carry a grudge, supposedly creating more animated hauntings in the town's historical buildings and cemeteries.

## WHEN BEING SINGLE WAS A CRIME

Salem isn't the only place that went through a hysterical witch-hunting phase. Suspected sorceress Lilias Adie was tortured and buried at low tide in the Firth of Forth estuary in Torryburn, Scotland. You can still see the half-ton slab they used as a grave topper to keep her in the ground, but, ironically, her bones aren't there. Grave robbers got them ages ago.

"LIFE AFTER DEATH, GHOSTS, PARADISE, ETERNITY—OF COURSE, WE TAKE ALL THAT AS GRANTED. OTHERWISE, WHERE'S THE FUN?"

—DENIS JOHNSON